International Arbitration of Renewable Energy Disputes

Second Edition

Authors
Emma Johnson, Lucy McKenzie and Matthew Saunders

Managing director
Sian O'Neill

International Arbitration of Renewable Energy Disputes, Second Edition
is published by
Globe Law and Business Ltd
3 Mylor Close
Horsell
Woking
Surrey GU21 4DD
United Kingdom
Tel: +44 20 3745 4770

www.globelawandbusiness.com

International Arbitration of Renewable Energy Disputes, Second Edition

ISBN 9781837230525
EPUB ISBN 9781837230532
Adobe PDF ISBN 9781837230549

Table of contents

Introduction

Climate change is an urgent concern. In December 2015, 196 parties signed the landmark Paris Agreement, committing to take action to limit the global temperature increase this century to well below 2°C and preferably to 1.5°C above pre-industrial levels. Energy policy is now well and truly mainstream in all the major economies, with 97 signatories to the United Nations Framework Convention on Climate Change adopting net zero pledges in 2023.[1] Despite this global commitment, the 2023 United Nations Environment Programme (UNEP) Emissions Gap Report shows that the world is way off target – heading, in fact, for a catastrophic temperature rise of 2.5°C above pre-industrial levels by the year 2100, even if all current Paris Agreement commitments are fully implemented (and we note that many of those commitments have in any event been caveated).[2] The targets are not yet out of reach; but to keep warming below 1.5°C, greenhouse gas emissions must fall by 42% by 2030.[3]

This calls for "immediate and unprecedented mitigation action" by all countries this decade.[4] There is wide consensus that the decarbonisation of the energy industry is critical to achieving the necessary "immediate and deep emission cuts".[5] At the same time, the energy industry must ensure it can meet increasing global demand (which is forecast to continue rising).[6] It must also take care that reliability of supply does not suffer – that when the sun does not shine or the wind does not blow, the lights will stay on. Battery and storage technology is increasingly important in that regard[7] and transition fuels such as natural gas have a major role to play – but electricity generation from renewable energy sources is the key to decarbonising the energy sector.

Governments worldwide recognise the importance of renewables. In 2023, the COP28 climate summit acknowledged that in order to keep the Paris Agreement target of 1.5°C alive, energy-related emissions must reach net zero by 2050.[8] To meet this objective, they set the goal of tripling global renewable energy capacity by 2030 and committed to transitioning away from fossil fuels.[9]

The necessary increase in renewables capacity is certainly achievable. In 2023, global renewable energy capacity increased by 473 gigawatts,[10] a faster increase in one year than at any time in the past three decades.[11] But there are nevertheless challenges in transitioning away from fossil fuels, and 2023 saw a series of global crises and events that forced governments to reconsider their energy supply and security, and look for ways to reduce their reliance on Russian oil and gas; so it raises the question whether the rapid increase in renewable energy capacity that year may have been an outlier.

Since this report was first published in 2021, the energy industry has seen substantial disruption. The COVID-19 pandemic resulted in severe supply chain disturbances; and the outbreak of war in Ukraine (and related imposition of sanctions on Russia) led to a global energy crisis, with the price of oil increasing dramatically, in turn putting pressure on energy prices worldwide. Ongoing conflict in the Middle East continues to put global energy markets at risk of further volatility.

These geopolitical events have caused states to place a focus on energy security. In many states this has involved directing attention to fossil fuel production – but there has also been accelerated renewables investment and deployment, given the strategic importance of renewables to the future of economic security. This growth trend is expected to continue: a survey conducted by Ashurst LLP in 2024, of more than 2,000 senior executives and managers involved in energy decision making at corporates throughout the G20, found that the vast majority (81%) of those corporates see investment in renewables as vital to their strategic growth.[12]

Players in the energy industry are facing pressure, not only from governments but also internally from their own boards and shareholders, to transition.[13] Many companies that have historically focused exclusively on traditional fuel sources are diversifying into the renewables sector. At the same time, the need for technological innovation in the sector offers particular opportunities for new entrants with smart ideas, or simply enough capacity to assist with the rapid growth in materials and component development required to meet supply chain demands.

The cost of renewable energy is rapidly decreasing as technologies (particularly solar) mature and benefit from mass production. As prices drop, the sector is expanding – global spending on renewables was US$735 billion in 2023[14] and renewable capacity additions are projected to grow to 7,300 GW by 2028.[15] Key government policies, including the Inflation Reduction Act in the United States, China's 14th Five-Year Plan for Renewable Energy and REPowerEU in the European Union, will further accelerate renewable electricity deployment. Particular attention will need to be given to infrastructure such as transmission networks, which are commonly 'in the wrong place' for renewables electricity generation, especially offshore wind.

Investment in renewable energy projects and underlying technologies will therefore continue to increase for the foreseeable future. The substantial infrastructure required, the development of new and innovative technologies, competition for materials and components, restrictions in supply chains and the state's role in encouraging

The cost of renewable energy is rapidly decreasing as technologies (particularly solar) mature and benefit from mass production.

investment through subsidies – whether through tariff structures or otherwise – all contribute to an increased risk of disputes. If not appropriately managed, these disputes could have significant adverse consequences. It will also remain the case that certain categories of renewable technologies are relatively untested and suffer technical performance and reliability challenges. Depending on how a renewables project is structured, disputes could impact, among other things:

- companies involved in the development, construction and operation of the project;
- developers of the underlying technology (including original equipment manufacturers and suppliers of key components including the raw materials and rare minerals used in various equipment);
- investors financing the project;
- offtakers of the electricity produced; and
- the sovereign states in which the project is located.

Stakeholders could find themselves embroiled in complex legal proceedings involving a multiplicity of laws, regulations and – crucially – business and governmental cultures.

Arbitration has long been the preferred forum for disputes arising out of international energy and construction projects and is a natural choice for disputes involving renewable energy projects. An understanding of the unique issues that arise in such projects and the protections available both under applicable contract law and international investment agreements (IIAs) and public international law, particularly against state action (or inaction), is crucial in mitigating the risk of disputes and maximising the prospects of success when disputes do arise. Those involved in renewables whose background is in the oil and gas world may be familiar with arbitration, but many will not be. And even those with a background in traditional fossil fuels will often not be attuned to the nuances that arise when arbitrating a renewable energy dispute. Effective use of international arbitration requires a measure of planning and forethought, and the purpose of this report is to assist with that.

This report is structured as follows:

- Chapter I introduces some of the main technologies and players in renewable energy projects.
- Chapter II considers the scope for renewables disputes to arise between private players and government entities and explains some of the key protections that exist at international law.
- Chapter III considers some of the unique features of renewables

projects that might require special consideration in order to manage and mitigate the risk of disputes arising (or to resolve them efficiently should that prove impossible), as well as some common sources of disputes in renewables projects.

- Chapter IV explains why international arbitration will often be the preferred forum for resolving renewable energy disputes.
- Chapter V draws together some of the lessons learned from our experience regarding key considerations for parties when drafting an arbitration agreement for a renewables project.
- Chapter VI suggests some 'top tips', based on our experience of advising and acting in renewables arbitrations, on how the tools of arbitration can best be deployed to prevent delay and promote efficient and effective resolution.
- Chapter VII considers possible trends in the types of disputes referred to arbitration in the future, and how arbitration might adapt to address them.

I. An introduction to renewables projects

1. What is renewable energy?

Renewable energy is energy derived from sources that are constantly replenished.[16] It includes energy derived from solar, wind, ocean, hydro, biomass and geothermal resources, as well as biofuels and hydrogen derived from renewable sources. A renewables project might combine these technologies with other power generation processes, such as the use of natural gas, to generate electricity, and might also incorporate energy storage technologies.

Some of the main renewable energy technologies that have reached relative commercial maturity are outlined below.[17] Renewables technologies are, however, continuing to evolve as expertise develops and companies experiment with new ideas.[18] Other forms of renewable electricity generation, including tidal technologies and novel ways of installing longer-standing renewable technologies such as floating offshore wind, are expected to reach commercial maturity and/or be deployed at scale this decade.[19]

Onshore wind

Wind power uses the kinetic energy from wind to generate electricity by rotating turbine blades, which turn a generator to produce electricity. Onshore wind power uses wind turbine generators installed on land to capture kinetic energy from wind. The turbines typically range from 1 to 3 megawatts (MW) in capacity. Onshore wind projects have a history of being more exposed to planning and regulatory approval issues. They can attract controversy at the planning stage because they can be seen from a distance (being typically constructed on hilltops where the wind is strongest); they are considered noisy; and they can interfere with bird migration and nesting. Although extreme weather conditions are risk factors that are more typically associated with offshore wind projects, climate change has made these relevant for onshore projects as well, as demonstrated by severe storms and wildfires across the United States.[20] Onshore wind turbines also frequently experience mechanical problems, which can lead to disputes.

Offshore wind

Offshore wind power uses wind turbine generators installed in the ocean or other bodies of water to capture kinetic energy from the wind to generate electricity. Electricity can be transmitted via subsea cables to an onshore substation and transferred to the distribution network. Wind speeds are higher and more consistent offshore than onshore, so larger turbines can be used. Offshore wind can therefore generate more energy per installed capacity than onshore wind. Offshore wind projects are also significantly more expensive than their onshore counterparts: post-COVID supply chain disruption, inflation and the rising cost of materials have led to a spate of new project cancellations in the United States.[21] In the United Kingdom, no bids at all were submitted at a government auction in 2023 because the prices set for electricity generated were too low to make the projects viable.[22] Particular risks attaching to offshore wind arise from the hostile environment in which the technology is placed – disputes arising from problems linked to corrosion have been widespread. Particular challenges also arise with floating (as opposed to fixed-bottom) offshore wind installations, and disputes are expected to become more common as more such projects come to fruition, not least because of the increased number of interfaces between the various structures required to be installed, and the fact that the technology has not yet been deployed at scale and was not designed for the specific purpose for which it is being used.[23]

Solar photovoltaics

Solar photovoltaic (PV) projects use cells made up of layers of semi-conducting material (usually silicon) to convert solar radiation into electricity. When solar radiation falls onto the cell, an electrical field is created across the layers which causes electrons to flow, generating electricity. A PV power plant contains many cells connected together in 'modules', with many modules forming 'strings' to produce electricity. Solar PV projects typically require large tracts of land and disputes may arise in connection with the impact of the project on adjacent properties or indigenous land rights and affected people.[24] There have also been instances of disputes arising out of the premature delamination of solar panels and other equipment problems like micro-cracking, as well as disputes concerning the failure of solar farms to meet their performance guarantees (not least because of the challenges in forecasting availability and production capacity, which are tied to specific weather conditions, with weather forecasting becoming increasingly challenging across the globe as a result of climate change).

Concentrated solar power

Concentrated solar power (CSP) uses lenses or mirrors to concentrate sunlight onto a single focal point. The energy is generally used to heat water to create superheated steam, which is then used to drive a turbine and produce electricity. There are a number of variations of CSP technology, including parabolic trough technology,[25] enclosed trough technology,[26] linear Fresnel reflector technology,[27] solar power tower technology[28] and dish engine or dish Stirling technology.[29] CSP technology is currently less prevalent than PV, given the higher costs associated with its installation, operation and maintenance. CSP allows for storage of energy, where suitable, through the use of various storage media such as molten salts. CSP and related storage technology is continuing to evolve and disputes have arisen in a number of projects as a result of operational difficulties.

Biomass

Biomass is fuel derived from organic matter, such as grasses, woodchips or crop waste products. Biomass projects are considered to produce a form of 'renewable' energy because the waste feedstock that is used to power them is replenishable. Electricity is generated by burning biomass fuels to release heat, which is generally used to produce steam and drive a turbine. Biomass plants do not suffer from the intermittency issues that affect solar and wind projects – but they do depend on the availability of a fuel supply and their output can be impacted by the quality of that fuel. Numerous disputes have arisen regarding the technology's varying ability to handle fuel of inconsistent quality.

2. The key players in renewables projects

The contractual structure to implement a renewable energy project will involve a number of different players and key contractual relationships. Some players will be private sector entities, often operating outside their home jurisdiction, while others will be regional and national governmental entities, subject to political control and often to national public law and administrative law regimes. In Chapters V and VI, we explain some of the key considerations flowing from the potential multi-party nature of renewables projects when drafting an arbitration clause and conducting proceedings.

2.1 The project company or consortium

At the centre of the contractual structure there will typically be a 'project company' or 'owner' (which might alternatively be known as the 'principal' or 'employer'). The project company will often be a special purpose vehicle (SPV) incorporated under the domestic law of the state in which the project is based, and may be owned by the project developer, as well as the project sponsors. It is important to give early consideration to the nationality of the shareholders of the project company. Foreign investors should take into account IIAs to which the host country is a party to ensure that their investment is protected under public international law, which will not be affected by any changes in domestic laws. We elaborate on this in Chapter II.

Alternatively, the investors in a project may choose not to incorporate an SPV, but rather participate in their individual capacities while working together as a consortium. The relationship between consortium entities will commonly be governed by a joint venture agreement, which might provide for each of the several consortium partners to perform discrete parts of the works. Disputes commonly arise between consortium members as to the extent to which each member has complied with its obligations and how and when those members are to be remunerated. The confidential nature of the arbitral process can be a significant advantage in such cases, where parties would prefer not to have their disputes made public.

2.2 The contractor(s)

The project company will typically engage one or more contractors to design and build the project (rather than doing so itself). It may choose to engage a single contractor on a 'turnkey' basis to take full responsibility for implementing the project. In our experience, this model is often used in solar power and biomass projects. The turnkey relationship is often defined in an 'engineering, procurement and

The project company will typically engage one or more contractors to design and build the project (rather than doing so itself). It may choose to engage a single contractor on a 'turnkey' basis to take full responsibility for implementing the project.

construction' (EPC) contract, which tasks the contractor with performing (or procuring the performance of) all design, civil works, manufacture and supply of equipment (including transportation to site), construction of the plant, installation and commissioning of equipment, and performance testing, such that when the contract is completed the project company has only to 'turn the key' to start a fully functioning and operational power plant. The contractor itself might choose to enter into sub-contracts with equipment manufacturers and other professional consultants and suppliers, in which case the project company might opt to maintain a direct contractual relationship with those subcontractors through a direct agreement, bank guarantee or other form of security. The turnkey approach is especially useful as a way of clarifying risk allocation in renewables projects involving immature technology.

Alternatively, a project company might prefer to adopt a 'multi-contract' model, directly contracting with a number of different subcontractors to design, supply, construct or install discrete items of equipment. In our experience, this model is often used in onshore and offshore wind projects where there is one contract for the supply, installation and commissioning of the turbine and a separate contract (or multiple contracts) for delivery of the balance of the plant. Floating offshore wind projects are particularly complex, and it is common that the turbine, floating substructure, anchoring and mooring systems, cabling and onshore substation (which all involve different engineering) are supplied by different parties under different contracts. In a multi-party contract structure like this, there are multiple interfaces at which pieces of equipment supplied by different contractors interact. This increased interaction can potentially lead to disputes involving multiple causes of loss or damage, raising questions as to which subcontractor is ultimately liable when something goes wrong, or who should bear responsibility and in what proportion. The scope for managing disputes that may arise under separate contracts but related subject matter therefore needs to be considered.

2.3 Operation and maintenance (O&M) provider

The relative immaturity of much renewables technology increases the challenges involved in predicting how it will operate over time. How such challenges are addressed contractually will typically be influenced by who has responsibility for O&M and whether this is undertaken by the owner or contractor or is outsourced. Unpredictability, inexperience and inconsistency as to O&M can rapidly impact upon the financial underpinnings of a project and become a source of complex, multilayered disputes.

2.4 The offtaker of energy produced

A power project structure will commonly include a long-term contract for the sale of electricity to a buyer (or 'offtaker'), known as a 'power purchase agreement' (PPA). The PPA counterparty may be a state-owned utility (which, in our experience, is more common in emerging economies, potentially bringing in local public law concerns) or a corporate entity. The PPA will generally contain terms for the sale of electricity – such as any applicable tariff or minimum volume of electricity to be supplied. The particular offtake arrangements will be affected by any regulatory regime for the supply of renewable energy in the jurisdiction in which a project is based, and can vary greatly. Most renewables projects generate revenue from selling the electricity they produce, but for certain projects (such as biomass projects) electricity sales can be a secondary source of revenue only – the project's main source of income might instead be government subsidies granted to renewable energy producers for units of renewable energy injected into the grid.

2.5 The state

The state hosting the renewables project plays an important role. Often, renewables projects are developed pursuant to a public–private partnership arrangement, with the state acting as a project sponsor or shareholder in the project company (either directly or through a state-owned company). Alternatively, private companies might commit to developing a project in a particular state as a result of financial incentives, such as subsidies. In any event it will usually be necessary to interact with the state in order to obtain the necessary licences and consents to develop the project, as well as to connect the project to the national grid in cases where the energy produced is to be used to meet local demand.

The Paris Agreement's system of Nationally Determined Contributions means that most states have made public commitments to generating a certain amount of energy from renewable sources by particular deadlines. Because of their political importance, renewables projects are often given 'trophy' or 'flagship' status by governments, meaning that they are in the spotlight, with greater exposure to scrutiny (not always from well-informed sources). This means there may be an additional political dynamic to disputes that arise in renewables projects that does not exist to the same degree in other construction and engineering disputes. Private sector players may find themselves more exposed to reputational risk, as well as greater pressure to deliver projects on time and on budget, than would exist in a conventional construction or engineering project. There may also be a great deal more scrutiny from civil society.

2.6 Funders

The costly infrastructure and long-term availability of resources required in renewable energy projects mean that such projects are typically sponsored and funded by a number of third parties. The project's sponsors (which may include a state or state-owned entity) will often own equity in the project company. In addition, the project company will commonly enter into a debt-financing relationship with one or a number of lenders, including banks, development finance institutions or international funders dedicated to addressing climate change, such as the Green Climate Fund in the case of renewables projects in developing countries.[30] In our experience, the law that governs the financing arrangements is typically chosen as the law governing the other project documents. Funders often retain rights in the project such that the project company must seek their permission before taking particular steps under the project contracts. For example, lender consent might be required before an initial acceptance certificate is issued, or before any claims are settled.

2.7 Insurers

The significant levels of capital investment involved in renewable energy projects mean that the project company, the contractor and the O&M contractor will normally take out insurance policies in respect of various risks associated with the project (including, for example, construction all-risk insurance, business interruption insurance, latent defects insurance and professional indemnity insurance). Accordingly, insurers are also important players in a renewable energy project. The potential interplay with insurers in circumstances where a dispute arises needs to be borne in mind, especially with regard to the creation of documentation that may be required to be produced in any related arbitration or litigation proceedings.

II. Renewables projects: international law protection

Renewable energy projects require significant upfront capital investment and are perceived as riskier investments than conventional power projects for a number of reasons, namely:

- the technology used has a limited proven track record;
- the pace of technological adaptation is fast; and
- the extended duration of projects makes them vulnerable to regulatory change.

It is widely accepted that the upscaling of investment in renewable energy technologies will largely come from foreign direct investment, particularly in developing economies.[31] In order to attract foreign direct investment, governments have historically offered support mechanisms to give investors sufficient revenue certainty to reflect the higher risk profile of the projects, and are likely to continue to do so in the future. Disputes have frequently arisen where changes are made to those support mechanisms that impact the viability of particular projects. Such changes are not uncommon, particularly as the cost of new technologies decreases over time, affecting the level of support that governments can reasonably offer to new projects, or simply because the political wind changes direction for myriad potential reasons.

The significant upfront investment required and the dependence of renewables projects on local laws for their successful operation and profitability – particularly where subsidies or other forms of government aid are involved – make it imperative that project developers and participants ensure that international law protection under IIAs is available. Early engagement with counsel in this respect is crucial.

1. International investment protection

1.1 Bilateral and multilateral investment treaties

IIAs typically take the form of bilateral investment treaties (BITs) and multilateral investment treaties (MITs). BITs are agreements between two states seeking to promote foreign direct investment by affording certain minimum standards of protection to foreign investors. Globally, nearly 3,000 BITs have been signed and around 2,200 are in force.[32] MITs are treaties between more than two states that provide similar protection. Important MITs for the protection of investments in the renewable energy industry include:

- the Energy Charter Treaty (ECT);[33]
- the United States–Mexico–Canada Agreement (USMCA) (which replaced the North American Free Trade Agreement (NAFTA) in 2020); and
- the Comprehensive and Progressive Agreement for Trans-Pacific Partnership (CPTPP).

The protections afforded by BITs and MITs generally apply only to 'investments' made in one contracting state by 'investors' of the other. Since the precise meaning of these terms depends on the words used in the applicable IIA, early engagement with counsel can ensure that foreign investment in a renewables project is made by a company that meets the requirements of an investor under a favourable IIA. Counsel can also assist with restructuring an existing investment so that treaty protection (or more favourable protection) can be secured.

The main advantage of IIAs is that the protection offered is independent of any applicable local laws. Therefore, while regulatory actions may be perfectly legal under the domestic law of the state where the project is located, an investor may nonetheless be entitled to compensation because the circumstances in which a regulatory change was introduced, or the manner in which it was implemented, violate the state's obligations under an IIA. Where a state-owned entity is one of the participants in the project, claims under an IIA may be available in addition to those under the relevant contract.

The protections afforded by BITs and MITs generally apply only to 'investments' made in one contracting state by 'investors' of the other.

1.2 The Energy Charter Treaty

For many years, the ECT has been the most significant MIT for the global energy industry. It is a widely ratified treaty that deals with investment and trade in the energy industry specifically, including renewable energy.[34]

The ECT was adopted in December 1994 and came into force on 16 April 1998. Its purpose is to provide a structural framework for the implementation of the principles of the 1991 European Energy Charter – namely to "catalyse economic growth by means of measures to liberalise investment and trade in energy".[35] As well as encouraging cross-border cooperation in the development of the energy sector, the ECT includes a number of commitments by signatory states to afford certain minimum standards of treatment to foreign investments made within their territories.

As of July 2024, there were around 50 contracting parties to the ECT.[36] However, a number of European states have recently withdrawn from the ECT or announced their intention to do so – the ramifications of this are discussed in section 3 below.

1.3 Substantive protections

The substantive protections contained in most IIAs, including the ECT, are broadly similar. IIAs protect qualifying 'investments' made by qualifying 'investors'. Under the ECT, the terms 'investment' and 'investor' are defined broadly and capture, for example, companies registered in a signatory state that hold shares directly or indirectly in a renewable energy project company incorporated in another signatory state.[37] The substantive protections in IIAs typically include the following:

Protection against expropriation without compensation

The protection against expropriation without compensation is a key feature of most IIAs.[38] Expropriation is not itself prohibited, but most IIAs (including the ECT) make the right to expropriate conditional. For an expropriation to be deemed legitimate, it must be:

- for a public purpose or a purpose "in the public interest";[39]
- non-discriminatory; and
- accompanied by prompt, adequate and effective compensation.

Certain MITs and BITs, including the ECT, also require that the expropriation is "carried out under due process of law".[40] The term has a much broader definition under public international law, such that a 'direct'[41] or 'indirect'[42] measure which negatively impacts a foreign investor's enjoyment of its investment (without compensation being paid) can give rise to a cause of action. For example, the tribunal in *Rockhopper v Italy* found that Italy had unlawfully expropriated the claimant's investment by denying its application for a production concession to exploit the Ombrina Mare oil field, awarding the investor nearly €200 million.[43]

Fair and equitable treatment

The obligation to accord fair and equitable treatment protects investors from measures or actions taken by host states that are arbitrary, grossly unfair or discriminatory against foreign investments in violation of their legitimate expectations.[44] This is the standard most frequently invoked in investor–state disputes,[45] and has been the basis of many of the arbitrations concerning changes to the renewable energy regulatory framework (by Spain, Italy, Czechia, Romania and Germany) brought by affected investors under the ECT. (These are discussed further in section 2, below.)

Protection against unreasonable and discriminatory measures

The ECT imposes an obligation on contracting states not to impair the management, maintenance, use, enjoyment or disposal of a foreign investment through "unreasonable or discriminatory measures".[46] This overlaps with the fair and equitable treatment standard but is a separate protection. Unreasonable or discriminatory measures are measures that are disproportionate to a state's intended policy objective, not founded in reason, or are based on discretion rather than legal standards, and which impair an investment. For example, in *ESPF v Italy*[47] an investor was awarded €16 million in compensation under the ECT following Italy's unreasonable unilateral modification of the specific commitments that induced the claimants to invest in Italy's renewable energy sector (tariffs set at a specific level for a period of 20 years).

Full protection and security

This standard imposes an obligation on host states of vigilance and due diligence to prevent damage to a protected investment, or to punish third parties for such damage or injury.[48] This protection might be relied on by an investor in circumstances where a host state has failed to prevent the physical destruction of property owned by the investor due to riots or similar physical attacks. The full protection and security standard has been invoked in investment cases where investors' property has been damaged in the course of the Libyan revolution[49] and in bomb attacks in Egypt associated with the fall of President Hosni Mubarak in 2011.[50]

No less favourable treatment, national treatment and most-favoured-nation treatment

Many IIAs including the ECT require a host state to afford treatment to foreign investors that is "no less favourable" to the treatment that state affords to foreign investors from other states, compared to investors who are nationals of the host state.[51] They essentially seek to preclude discriminatory treatment as between different investors.

Adherence to obligations entered into by the state

Some IIAs such as the ECT include an 'umbrella' clause that imposes a duty on states to comply with any 'obligations' entered into with protected investors. Umbrella clauses elevate breaches of obligations entered into by a state outside of the IIA to breaches of the IIA, enabling investors to access the remedies available under the IIA (including arbitration against the state). The relevant obligations are usually in a contract (such as a PPA) between an investor and a state-owned entity but, in particular cases, can include obligations imposed by legislation or regulations. For example, the *ESPF v Italy* decision concerned offers made by Italy of guaranteed 20-year feed-in tariffs to investors in the solar energy industry who met specific criteria. The tribunal concluded that these offers made to specific identifiable entities constituted an 'obligation' on Italy's part for the purposes of the umbrella clause in the ECT and that, in violating those offers, Italy had breached the umbrella clause.[52]

1.4 Reference to arbitration

Most of the BITs and MITs signed to date, including the ECT, provide for international arbitration as the mechanism for resolving disputes. The mere ability of an investor to raise claims directly against a state before an independent and international tribunal, outside the domestic judicial framework, can itself be a useful means of exerting leverage short of commencing formal proceedings.

The ECT offers three arbitration options:

- International Centre for Settlement of Investment Disputes (ICSID) arbitration;
- *ad hoc* arbitration under the Arbitration Rules of the United Nations Commission on International Trade Law (UNCITRAL) ('the UNCITRAL Rules'); and
- Stockholm Chamber of Commerce (SCC) arbitration.[53]

Other IIAs provide for alternative arbitration forums, including the Permanent Court of Arbitration (PCA) and the International Chamber of Commerce (ICC).

In practice, most investment disputes are filed with ICSID, which is a self-contained system available to states that are parties to the

In practice, most investment disputes are filed with ICSID, which is a self-contained system available to states that are parties to the Convention on the Settlement of Investment Disputes between States and Nationals of Other States.

Convention on the Settlement of Investment Disputes between States and Nationals of Other States ('the ICSID Convention').[54] ICSID also has an Additional Facility which provides for ICSID arbitration in circumstances where only one of the parties is a contracting state to the ICSID Convention (or a national of such a state). ICSID's relationship with the World Bank means that states that are dependent on the World Bank for financial support may be less likely to ignore arbitral awards rendered under ICSID's auspices.

2. The renewables cases against Spain, Italy, Czechia, Romania and Germany

The importance of IIA protection in renewables projects is amply demonstrated by numerous cases against Spain, Italy, Czechia, Romania and Germany stemming from regulatory changes introduced by those states reducing the financial support afforded to investors in renewables projects. The claims have primarily involved alleged breaches of the fair and equitable treatment standard, unreasonable or discriminatory measures and indirect expropriation.

Spain had introduced an electricity incentive scheme in 2004, seeking to attract foreign direct investment in renewable energy sources, which included incentives and subsidies for solar energy. In 2007, Royal Decree 661/2007 was introduced, providing for regulated tariffs and premiums on top of the market price for electricity produced from solar energy. However, for a number of reasons (including, in part, the global financial crisis), Spain experienced a severe tariff deficit which, by 2012, had reached about €25 billion. To address the deficit, the government implemented changes to its subsidy regime, including eliminating the tariff system with retroactive effect, eliminating premium payments, and imposing a 7% tax on electricity generation. The reductions caused a number of foreign investors in the solar industry to seek relief under the ECT. To date, more than 50 arbitration claims are known to have been pursued by foreign investors against Spain as a result of these changes.[55] Of those, awards on the merits have been handed down in at least 36 cases, with six finding in favour of the state[56] and 30 finding in favour of the investor.[57] In general, investors have been successful where they could point to a specific commitment that was made to them (giving rise to legitimate expectations as to the stability of the regulatory regime),[58] or the tribunal considered that the regulatory changes made were so radical and unexpected as to transform the legal environment surrounding the investment.[59] Spain has, however, not yet paid any of the damages ordered against it pursuant to these awards.

Italy offered incentives for solar energy generation from 2003 as part of its Energy Account Regime, which included feed-in tariffs and a legislative minimum price at which the state-owned energy company would purchase electricity from renewable energy producers. In 2013, the minimum price incentives were repealed, and in 2014 the feed-in tariffs were reduced. More than 10 arbitration proceedings have been commenced under the ECT and other investment treaties by affected investors.[60] Investors have been less successful in these cases than in the Spanish cases and, to date, only three investors have succeeded, in cases where they could demonstrate that a specific commitment was made to them.[61]

In 2005, Czechia introduced a feed-in tariff for solar-generated electricity sold directly to grid operators, which could not be reduced by more than 5% per year. The government also introduced an income tax exemption for renewable energy producers. Then, in 2011, the government imposed a retroactive 26% tax on the electricity output of solar power plants commissioned in 2009 and 2010, to be applied for three years, at the end of which the tax was reduced to 10% and its application limited to plants commissioned in 2010.[62] The government also passed legislation authorising a faster reduction in the tariff rate, and abolished the income tax exemption. To date, seven arbitration proceedings are known to have been commenced by foreign investors in the solar sector affected by these changes, alleging breaches of the ECT and other BITs.[63] Czechia has been successful in six cases,[64] the tribunals finding that the changes were clearly aimed at addressing a public interest matter, and that the state's conduct with regard to the changes was reasonable and proportionate.[65]

Romania has also faced a flurry of claims under the ECT following changes to the incentive scheme it built to attract investment in its renewable energy sector.[66] Further to its Paris Agreement commitments, Romania passed a law requiring energy sector producers to purchase 'green certificates' for every megawatt hour of power sold. These certificates were issued to qualifying renewable energy producers based on the amount of electricity they fed into the grid; they could then on-sell the certificates directly to other producers or trade them on the green certificates market. Between 2011 and 2014, Romania introduced a series of reforms reducing the number of green certificates issued, then in September 2017 introduced further changes, including limiting the number of times the green certificates could be sold. Investors in Romania's renewables industry have argued that these changes effectively "destroyed the demand for the incentives mechanism" in Romania in breach of Romania's obligation to accord fair and equitable treatment to investors.[67] To date, one tribunal has awarded compensation to an investor, finding that Romania's changes drastically altered the essential characteristics of the incentive scheme, in breach of its ECT commitments.[68]

Germany introduced an amendment to its renewable energy law in 2017 requiring investors in offshore wind projects to participate in a public tariff auction process, whereby the cheapest rate for the consumer on offer would be successful. Two claims have been filed against Germany under the ECT, with investors arguing that the auction process effectively excluded projects that were not sufficiently advanced from consideration, forcing them to abandon the offshore wind projects they had in development.[69] No decisions on the merits have yet been issued in these cases.

3. A word of warning: ECT withdrawals

In 2023 and 2024 a number of European states either withdrew from the ECT or confirmed their intention to do so. These states include France, Spain, Germany, Poland, Luxembourg, Slovenia, the Netherlands, Denmark, Ireland, Portugal and the United Kingdom. The European Union and Euratom have also notified their withdrawal.

The withdrawing states have expressed concerns that the ECT was impeding the energy transition by disincentivising governments from legislating to promote the transition away from fossil fuels. There is a perception amongst these states that, as parties to the ECT, they would be likely to face significant damages claims from investors in

Germany introduced an amendment to its renewable energy law in 2017 requiring investors in offshore wind projects to participate in a public tariff auction process, whereby the cheapest rate for the consumer on offer would be successful.

traditional fossil fuel projects as a consequence of efforts to address climate change concerns and transition towards low or no carbon energy systems. In fact, statistics show that the bulk of claims brought under the ECT to date have been by investors in the renewables sector, in particular those discussed above against Spain, Italy, Czechia, Romania and Germany, rather than by investors in the coal, oil or gas sectors. Attempts at modernising the ECT to address these concerns got as far as an agreement in principle in June 2022 but are now at an impasse as a result of the withdrawals.

The withdrawals have also been driven by the European Commission's attempts to eliminate investor–state arbitration in Europe. In 2018, the Court of Justice of the European Union (ECJ) found that investor–state arbitration clauses in intra-EU BITs violate EU law.[70] In 2021, the ECJ extended that finding specifically to the ECT, and ruled that the arbitration clause in the ECT was incompatible with EU law.[71] Since then, arbitral tribunals have largely rejected jurisdictional objections raised by states based on the ECJ's findings,[72] but certain European domestic courts (in particular in Sweden) have annulled or refused to enforce intra-EU arbitration awards.[73] As a consequence, the viability of intra-EU investment treaty arbitration – and whether investors will ultimately obtain an award that can be enforced – is uncertain.

The withdrawal of EU member states from the ECT obviously impacts those investing in the energy sector of the withdrawing states (or, indeed in the European Union more generally). Because of the reciprocal nature of the commitments contained within the ECT, the withdrawals also remove the protections available to those investors who are nationals of a withdrawing state, and who have energy sector investments in other ECT states. In many instances, recourse to national courts (frequently the only alternative to investment arbitration) has been shown to be a problematic option where significant changes to subsidy regimes have impacted negatively upon renewables projects.

Those with existing investments covered by the ECT will likely continue to be protected for a further 20 years under the sunset provision of the ECT, although there is at present some debate about whether the sunset provision should also be rescinded. In this regard, in June 2024 the European Union and 26 member states signed a declaration and *inter se* agreement seeking to disapply the ECT's sunset clause in respect of intra-EU disputes. The practical effect of this agreement on arbitration claims (and indeed whether it is enforceable as a matter of international law) is yet to be seen – quite how states that have withdrawn from a treaty can subsequently seek to amend its provisions is uncertain.

Investors with potential intra-EU claims should monitor developments and consider whether they have enforcement options outside the European Union (where domestic courts have been more willing to enforce intra-EU awards than European courts), or whether they should seek to restructure their investments to obtain alternative private and public international law protections. Alternative ways of protecting intra-EU investments against regulatory risk might include:

- considering whether contractual mechanisms can be negotiated to maximise protection, for example, inclusion of an appropriate stabilisation clause (stabilisation clauses are discussed in more detail in Chapter III);
- considering whether there are any BITs that provide protection as an alternative to the ECT, ideally with a non-EU member state. Where BITs are not available as a function of the existing corporate structure behind an investment, investors might consider restructuring to maximise protection (restructuring is typically permissible before a specific dispute arises but might arguably constitute an abuse of process if carried out once a dispute is foreseeable); and
- taking steps towards commencing arbitration proceedings under the ECT (including by sending notices of dispute and commencing cooling-off periods) as soon as possible, before the withdrawals take effect and the sunset provision terminates.

While renewables projects are similar in many respects to other large construction and engineering projects, they do have some distinctive features that can lead to disputes and complicate their resolution, in particular the relatively untried and untested technology and the remote locations often involved.

III. Common areas of dispute and contractual protections

Most disputes arising from renewables projects are more likely to result in contractual claims rather than claims under an IIA. Disputes can arise from a variety of sources when constructing and operating a renewable energy project. While renewables projects are similar in many respects to other large construction and engineering projects, they do have some distinctive features that can lead to disputes and complicate their resolution, in particular the relatively untried and untested technology and the remote locations often involved.

It is important to understand the defining characteristics of a renewable energy project in order to adopt a robust contractual framework that maximises the chance of avoiding disputes, while facilitating the efficient resolution of those that cannot be avoided. Some of the unique characteristics of renewables projects that provide scope for disputes are discussed below (section 1), together with the types of disputes that can arise (sections 2 and 3) and how commercial disputes risk might be mitigated at the contracting stage (section 4).

1. Unique characteristics of renewables projects and the scope for disputes

1.1 Multiple players and contracts

Given the number of different players and contracts in a renewables project (see Chapter I), it is important to understand and account for the competing interests and commercial motivations that might be at play in any dispute. Contractual obligations or avenues for relief might exist not only in the particular agreement from which the dispute arises, but in other contracts such as:

- a direct agreement between the project company and a subcontractor or supplier;
- an interface agreement between a construction contractor and an O&M contractor; or
- a collateral warranty agreement with a manufacturer.

The project's lenders may have retained key rights in the project, such as the approval of material changes to contract terms or the engagement of contractors, manufacturers and suppliers, or they may have 'step-in' or 'cure' rights recorded in direct agreements with the project's construction contractor(s) or O&M contractor. Furthermore, there may be an alternative avenue of relief available under a policy of insurance – parties should give early consideration to whether any insurance policy might respond to a potential claim.

It may be that the project company has back-to-back obligations, both to fulfil and to receive, up and down the contractual chain, and is therefore able to pass on any contractual claim against it. In this case, it will be important to consider how to proceed in the event of a dispute. A party might be in a stronger position if it first pursues proceedings against one party and secures a determination, before commencing proceedings against the other; but in doing so may risk falling foul of limitation periods or inconsistent awards (on the basis that arbitration awards do not bind non-parties). Alternatively, it may be prudent to seek to join additional parties to the dispute, or to consolidate a number of related disputes into the same action so that a determination can be made binding all parties at once. (Joinder and consolidation are explained in further detail in Chapter V; they are seldom straightforward in international arbitration.) It will also be important to ensure that a position is not advanced in one dispute that is inconsistent with a position taken in another. Early engagement of counsel can be invaluable in increasing the likelihood that relevant documents will attract legal privilege and, therefore, immunity from production or disclosure in any formal legal proceeding.

1.2 New and emerging technology

Some renewables technologies, such as solar photovoltaic and onshore wind, have been in commercial use for decades and are tried and tested. Other technologies are new and experimental, or are being deployed at scales never before seen as countries look to achieve their net zero targets. For example, technologies such as floating offshore wind and tidal systems are relatively new, particularly when deployed at an industrial scale. Renewables projects can also incorporate new technologies into more established ones (such as the addition of batteries or thermal energy storage technologies to solar projects, or the incorporation of steam or gas turbines into solar or hybrid projects).

The use of new and emerging technologies, coupled with the speed at which renewables projects are often rolled out (to achieve grid connection in time to qualify for subsidies and allow governments to make good on their net zero promises), can lead to unforeseen and unprecedented problems during the construction or operation phases of a renewables project when it transpires that the technology does not work as successfully as anticipated. The pace of technological change as energy transition progresses means this situation is unlikely to change any time soon. It may be possible to cater for such circumstances by including appropriately worded *force majeure* or

Early engagement of counsel can be invaluable in increasing the likelihood that relevant documents will attract legal privilege and, therefore, immunity from production or disclosure in any formal legal proceeding.

contractual protections (where the applicable law does not provide such relief). Identifying which technology is new and getting clarity up front about how to measure its performance is an important consideration. Should a dispute be foreshadowed, lining up an expert to explain the shortcomings to a tribunal (and even provide early input into the legal strategy) is key, but can be difficult given the relatively small pool of available experts.

1.3 No standardised contracts and the lack of precedent

Suites of standardised contracts are common in the mining, petroleum and construction industries, often developed by institutions such as the Association of International Energy Negotiators (AIEN, formerly AIPN, the Association of International Petroleum Negotiators), the Australian Mining and Petroleum Law Association (AMPLA) and the International Federation of Consulting Engineers (FIDIC). As a consequence, there is an established body of guidance and jurisprudence as to how these contracts are to be interpreted, which can provide certainty and go some way towards avoiding (or resolving) disputes.[74]

However, the renewables industry does not yet have an established set of international standardised contracts. Some progress has been made towards the development of standard contracts in the solar industry (the International Renewable Energy Agency (IRENA) and the Terrawatt Initiative, for example, have produced a series of standardised contracts for small and medium-sized grid-connected solar PV projects)[75] and in the wind industry (the International Marine Contractors Association has published a standard contract for transport and installation works in offshore wind projects[76] and FIDIC has announced that it is developing a new contract specifically for offshore wind projects[77]). There is not yet, however, any equivalent to the suite of standard form contracts that exists in the mining, petroleum and construction industries.

The effect is that the contracts for renewables projects that we have seen are similar in structure, but vary greatly in terms of detail. In our experience, it is not unusual for renewables contracts to be based on construction industry *pro forma* contracts, in particular those developed by FIDIC, but heavily amended to account for renewables-specific risks (such as the risk of adverse weather conditions affecting an offshore wind project). The act of amending a standard form contract can itself give rise to disputes, and the fact that such contracts are not yet standard form in their application to renewables projects means there is less certainty as to how they might be interpreted by a court or tribunal. It is therefore important that any amendments to standard forms are made with the assistance and advice of legal counsel experienced in the nuances of renewables projects.

1.4 New industry players

The increasing global focus on renewables is putting renewed pressure on engineering and construction companies already involved in the sector. As a result, many new and less experienced players are bidding to enter the industry. These newer players may underbid to win work, leading to situations where contractors with a relative lack of experience find they need to claw back value by making extension of time and variation claims, which are often disputed. Sponsors and stakeholders might also find that the operational and financial assumptions underpinning their investments have been inadequately informed and overambitious. This will be a further likely source of dispute.

1.5 Regulatory landscape in flux

Renewables projects tend to be long term in nature, simply because it can take a number of years, even decades, for a project to generate enough revenue to make up for the high upfront capital costs of investment. The long life of renewables projects exposes them to the risk of changes to the applicable regulatory landscape. This risk is particularly high for renewables projects, as states are actively legislating to incentivise investment in the renewables sector as a means of furthering the energy transition. One key pressure point imposed by the regulatory landscape is the need to achieve grid connection by a certain time in order to be eligible for subsidies or to enable the state to meet net zero targets. That time pressure can lead to claims. Moreover, as project costs continue to come down, many of the financial incentive schemes in place will prove to be unsustainable and subject to change by the host state as government budgets inevitably come under stress and scrutiny. Investor-state recourse may be a possibility where a change in the regulatory landscape negatively impacts a project. Commercial claims might be pursued under the relevant construction or operating contract, or PPA.

1.6 Unpredictability of the weather

Many renewables projects are heavily dependent on advantageous weather conditions; and adverse weather can affect the availability of installations and their resulting ability to produce the amount of energy originally anticipated and contracted for. The remote locations in which many renewables projects are built (eg, in the middle of a desert, a body of water, or offshore) mean that adverse weather conditions can cause delay to transportation of key materials and equipment and the project's construction more generally. Even once the project has started operating, unexpected weather conditions can negatively impact the amount of electricity produced, potentially undermining its ability to meet its contractual performance guarantees and leading to disputes concerning responsibility for the lower than anticipated performance. As global weather conditions

The domestic law of the place where a project is built is generally of greater relevance to renewables projects than it is to traditional fossil fuel projects. The reason is that in the case of renewables projects, electricity is usually injected into the grid of the country in which it is generated, in contrast to many oil and gas projects, where fuel is extracted and exported over great distances and across international borders.

continue to be unpredictable, and even volatile, as a result of climate change, these types of disputes are only likely to become more frequent.

1.7 Vulnerability to supply chain disruption

The international nature of renewables projects and their dependence on specific raw materials (such as the critical minerals needed to manufacture solar panels and wind turbine generators) make them particularly vulnerable to problems arising from disruption to supply chains. The sensitivity of the energy industry to geopolitical factors has been amply demonstrated in recent years, as traditional trade routes were disrupted by the COVID-19 pandemic and international conflicts. Rocketing energy prices and inflation rates have also resulted in the manufacturing costs associated with renewables projects escalating. Supply chain cost increases and supply disruption cause delay and add cost to projects, leading to disputes as to who bears the risk of such additional time and cost.

1.8 Relevance of local law

The domestic law of the place where a project is built is generally of greater relevance to renewables projects than it is to traditional fossil fuel projects. The reason is that in the case of renewables projects, electricity is usually injected into the grid of the country in which it is generated, in contrast to many oil and gas projects, where fuel is extracted and exported over great distances and across international borders.[78] There may also be mandatory provisions of local laws, such as hardship provisions, that would apply regardless of the terms of the contract and its governing law. The effect is that national laws, particularly national environmental policies, are more likely to be relevant to renewables projects, and might be an issue in the future in the context of mitigation steps taken by states to deal with climate change, positively or negatively.

2. Common disputes in the main phases of a renewables project

The unique characteristics of renewables projects discussed in the previous section tend to give rise to disputes in each of the three main phases of a project:

- the development phase;
- the construction phase; and
- the operational phase.

We shall now look at disputes that are common, in our experience, in each of these project phases.

2.1 Disputes in the development phase

The development phase involves obtaining any licences, permissions or consents required for the installation of the project. These might include, for example, environmental assessments, planning consents, regulatory consents, land use agreements, land clearances or road-widening permits to transport large items of equipment. Renewables projects have been known to face problems in obtaining planning consent. For example, onshore wind projects may face opposition due to their visual impact, noise pollution and potential interference with bird migration and nesting. Offshore wind projects have faced difficulties in achieving environmental impact assessment approval because of the need for a comprehensive analysis of the seabed and local currents, as well as the relatively unknown long-term impact of the technology on the marine environment, including noise, water quality and sediment management issues, and the impact on marine birdlife and even airport approach paths and military radar coverage.[79] The involvement of state entities can significantly increase the bureaucracy associated with implementing the project, especially where new technology is involved. A source of disputes in the development phase is, therefore, delay in obtaining the necessary permissions. Issues of local administrative law relevant to the granting of permits may also arise, and early engagement of local counsel is a priority in this respect.

In certain circumstances, IIAs may offer relief where loss arises due to the state's conduct in issuing relevant environmental and other approvals. For example, an investment treaty claim was successfully brought by an affected investor against Canada, arising from the refusal of the environmental authority to issue Renewable Energy Approvals due to the unknown potential effects of offshore wind development.[80] The issuance of the approvals was a condition precedent to allowing offshore wind projects commissioned by the government of Ontario to proceed, and the failure to obtain the approvals on a number of projects resulted in suspension of the government's Feed-in Tariff Program in 2011, pending further scientific research.[81]

Disputes in the development phase may also arise as a result of supply chain disruption or geopolitical factors increasing the cost of projects. For example, in late 2023 a number of offshore wind projects in Europe and the United States were cancelled due to inflation and supply chain disruption increasing the cost of implementing the projects and making the originally agreed prices no longer viable.[82] Where a project is cancelled, disputes may arise concerning the amount payable on cancellation – termination and liquidated and unliquidated damages claims are also likely to follow.

2.2 Disputes in the construction phase

The construction phase in a typical power plant project involves the

Renewables projects have been known to face problems in obtaining planning consent. For example, onshore wind projects may face opposition due to their visual impact, noise pollution and potential interference with bird migration and nesting.

construction, manufacture, delivery to site, installation, commissioning and initial testing of the plant and all key pieces of equipment, together with the associated civil works. When the plant is capable of generating electricity, it is connected to the grid. This point is variously referred to as 'initial acceptance', 'taking over', 'substantial completion' or 'initial commercial operation'.

Delay is again a significant source of disputes in the construction phase. The contract for delivery of a renewables project typically requires key milestones to be achieved by specified dates to prevent delays and cost overruns. The contractor's commitment to meet those deadlines is usually secured by an obligation to pay a contractually specified amount (known as 'liquidated damages') for each day that the project is delayed. Disputes may arise where a contractor challenges the levying of liquidated damages; either because it claims an extension of time, or it challenges the provision itself is as an unenforceable penalty (this is discussed further in section 4.5 below).

Construction may be delayed for an infinite number of reasons. Renewables projects are often constructed in remote locations (given the need for access to large tracts of land and the relevant natural resource) which can cause delays in mobilising personnel and equipment. Problems might arise when installing foundations and export cables on the seabed in largely unknown conditions, or more generally from the severe environment where the project is being built. The restrictions on transport and employment imposed by governments in response to the COVID-19 pandemic and the rise in manufacturing costs attributable to energy market volatility resulting from the Russia–Ukraine war and related imposition of sanctions are paradigm examples of circumstances that can delay construction. Such delays might be excused under *force majeure* or hardship provisions, depending on how clauses have been drafted and the applicability of any law that recognises a hardship doctrine.

Disputes commonly arise in relation to claims for costs arising out of a change in the contractor's agreed scope of works, typically regarding whether or not there has in fact been such a change. For example, an instruction to change the design of a boiler in a biomass project might fall within the original scope of works on the basis that the initial design provided by the contractor was defective.

Disputes concerning defects and quality issues are particularly common and are based upon requirements that the works meet certain contractual standards of quality (for example, that on completion they are fit for purpose or meet the requisite design life).

Disputes commonly arise in relation to claims for costs arising out of a change in the contractor's agreed scope of works, typically regarding whether or not there has in fact been such a change.

Given the scale and technical nature of the equipment used in renewables projects, there is ample scope for problems concerning quality to arise, and for uncertainty as to durability where immature technologies are involved. Key pieces of equipment may fail – for example, PV modules may malfunction or degrade, or undersea cables may be damaged during installation. There may also be failures in design, manufacture or construction: an offshore wind turbine foundation may fail to comply with industry-standard corrosion protections; a boiler may not tolerate the chemical make-up of the feedstock in a biomass plant; or solar panels might develop micro-fractures. Assessing compliance with contractual standards of quality can be a difficult exercise when there is little established track record to which to refer, as is the case with many renewable technologies. In a dispute scenario, a careful choice of supporting expert analysis may enable helpful comparisons with other similar technologies or with similar equipment used in other applications.

A further source of dispute is the analysis of a plant's long-term performance. A contract for the implementation of a renewables project might require the plant's performance to be tested over a period of time and compared against agreed guaranteed levels of performance. It is not unusual for a contract to require a contractor to pay liquidated damages to the owner where it cannot be demonstrated that the plant is capable of achieving those guaranteed performance levels. Disputes might arise as to how the plant's performance is to be measured for the purpose of these tests or whether any required tests have been completed successfully. Other guaranteed levels of performance might also be agreed upon. For example, a biomass project might contain an output guarantee; or a wind project might include a 'mechanical availability' guarantee. Disputes might arise as to the underlying cause of any failure to meet the guarantees – for example, whether the failure of a biomass plant to perform is attributable to a defective boiler design or out-of-specification feedstock; or whether a solar farm's failure to perform is caused by a defective design or a failure to keep the panels free of dust, sand or snow.

2.3 Disputes in the operation phase

The operation phase starts when the plant commences commercial operation, exporting electricity to the grid. If the project company has engaged an O&M contractor to manage the day-to-day running of the plant, the contractor's obligations will usually commence at this point. The scope for disputes in the operational phase is also broad; and exacerbated by the long operational life of renewables projects.

Disputes may include whether or not an O&M contractor is entitled to additional payment as a consequence of changes in scope – the contractor might, for example, seek payment for work that falls outside its defined list of activities, such as works to 'upgrade' the project that go beyond 'maintenance'. As the profit margins of renewable energy companies decline, operators may be more inclined to pursue such claims than they were previously.

Political factors might change the legal landscape surrounding the project in the course of its operational life, including the introduction of laws requiring a percentage of the plant's operational personnel to be nationals, or that the plant uses a certain proportion of local suppliers. A dispute might arise as to whether the operator is entitled to additional payment as a consequence of these changes.

The relationship between an O&M contractor and construction contractor(s) in the operational phase can lead to disputes. In this period, the O&M contractor has day-to-day responsibility for the operation of the plant, but the construction contractor may have continuing obligations as regards defects rectification or performance testing. Disputes commonly arise in this phase as to whether problems at the plant constitute defects (for which the contractor is responsible) or are issues of operation and maintenance (for which the O&M contractor is responsible).

3. Other areas of dispute

Disputes also arise outside the main project phases described above, more broadly as a consequence of the energy transition. Other potential categories of dispute that might impact a renewables project include:

- price adjustment disputes;
- joint venture disputes;
- bribery and corruption allegations;
- greenwashing claims;
- carbon credits and trading disputes; and
- financing disputes.

3.1 Price adjustment disputes

Given the heavy dependence of renewables projects on the broad array of equipment, electrical components and raw materials used to produce them, disputes can arise where a supplier seeks to adjust the price it is owed by the contractor for its supplies in response to, for example, inflationary pressures or commodity market volatility. Disputes might also arise if the contractor in turn seeks to pass on any price increase to the employer, or project company.

Where the applicable contract includes a price escalation or a price review clause (as to which see section 4.6 below), a price adjustment can be relatively straightforward to enforce. Disputes can, however, arise regarding whether or not the contractual mechanism has been triggered, whether notice provisions have been satisfied, or how the adjustment itself is to be calculated. Where there is no contractual price review provision, companies may need to consider whether contractual *force majeure*, change in law or hardship clauses apply, or whether similar concepts (such as doctrines of hardship in civil law systems) apply. Counsel can advise on potential avenues of relief in these scenarios.

3.2 Joint venture disputes

As explained in Chapter I, it is common for a number of companies to band together in a consortium or joint venture to deliver a renewables project. The relationship between these joint venture parties is usually recorded in a joint venture agreement or shareholders agreement. There is ample scope for disputes to arise between joint venturers as a project progresses. Deadlocks can arise where the joint venture contract (or articles of association) requires decisions to be made unanimously and board members cannot agree. Disputes might also arise where one joint venturer is in default, such as by failing to contribute its share of funds or making unauthorised changes to its ownership or control. The contract might contain a mechanism for resolving any such disputes or deadlocks outside formal legal proceedings, but in our experience joint venture disputes can and regularly do end up requiring intervention by a court or a tribunal to resolve matters.

3.3 Bribery and corruption allegations

Renewables projects have been recognised by global working groups as particularly vulnerable to bribery and corruption risk given the high capital investment required to implement them, the lucrative contracts on offer, the role of governments and the speed at which such projects need to be rolled out to meet climate change objectives.[83] Thorough due diligence is critical to reduce the risk of reputational damage (including by association with other companies in the project chain who might be implicated in wrongdoing). Appropriate warranties and indemnities might also be sought.

3.4 Greenwashing claims

Renewable energy companies should be conscious of potential greenwashing claims, whereby companies are pursued for making misleading statements to the public about their environmental credentials. Such claims are on the rise given the increased global focus on climate change. For example, in 2021 a case was filed in the Federal Court of Australia alleging that an oil and gas company had engaged in misleading or deceptive conduct by claiming that natural gas is a "clean fuel" that provides "clean energy". This was claimed to misrepresent the true effect of natural gas on the climate.[84] Companies should be careful not to overstate a project's environmental credentials, and conscious of statements made by any relevant third parties (such as sponsors or subcontractors) regarding the project.

3.5 Carbon credits and trading disputes

Many countries have introduced carbon credits or emissions trading schemes allowing companies to earn credits for renewable electricity generation which can be traded on the energy markets. Purchasing carbon credits can be a popular way for companies to meet (or move towards) net zero targets. Disputes can arise from contracts for the sale and purchase of carbon credits, particularly regarding the value of the credits or the termination of the contract. For example, one party may decide not to proceed on the basis that the deal is no longer an attractive proposition. A project company might also seek redress against a contractor where the project, as built, does not qualify for carbon credits that it assumed would apply, and based upon which the investment in the project was made.

3.6 Financing disputes

In addition to the kinds of dispute that typically arise with any financed construction project, disputes relating to the financing of renewables projects might arise where a project fails to meet technical specifications or guarantees under the financing contracts, or contractual sustainability criteria.

4. Contractual protections to mitigate disputes risk

Given the potential areas of dispute, renewable industry participants should consider what options are available to them to mitigate their potential exposure. Proper investment treaty planning is important, and investors should consider whether there is a chain of ownership to an entity that qualifies for investment protection under an applicable treaty in place. If not, it may be possible to restructure an investment to attract such protection. Counsel can assist in this respect.

In addition, companies should consider what contractual protections are available. It is generally possible to mitigate the risk of disputes arising in renewables projects through appropriately worded contractual protections. Some common protections are discussed below.

4.1 Stabilisation clauses

Investment in a renewables project is often made under an investment contract between a state and a foreign investor, typically structured as a concession agreement or a PPA. The substantial upfront investment is made based on the regulatory regime in place at the time the 'final

Many countries have introduced carbon credits or emissions trading schemes allowing companies to earn credits for renewable electricity generation which can be traded on the energy markets. Purchasing carbon credits can be a popular way for companies to meet (or move towards) net zero targets.

investment decision' (FID) is taken. However, the political wind may change and subsequent government policies, particularly where they involve subsidies, tariffs or other forms of government support, may render the investment an unattractive proposition. Where the government is the counterparty to the investment contract, it may be possible for contracts to minimise such risks through stabilisation clauses. These clauses broadly fall into five categories:[85]

- 'Freezing clauses' are intended to freeze key aspects of national legislation, such as tax or environmental provisions, that affect the investor for the life of the investment. These clauses typically provide that legislation enacted subsequent to the investment contract will not bind the investor.
- 'Intangibility clauses' provide that a host government cannot unilaterally nationalise a project or modify an investment contract. Any changes require the consent of the investor.
- 'Economic equilibrium' or 'rebalancing the benefits' clauses provide protection by ensuring that, in the event of a change of law that adversely affects the investor, the host government will ensure that the investor is not financially disadvantaged. Modern stabilisation clauses invariably take this form.
- An 'allocation of burden' clause is similar to an economic equilibrium clause and provides that the burden of a change in

legislation will be met by the host state. For example, in the oil and gas industry, a production-sharing contract might stipulate that the burden of any tax changes will be carried by the state oil company rather than the private investor.

- 'Hybrid' clauses contain elements of two or more of these different types of stabilisation clause.

4.2 Performance guarantees and minimum standards of performance

Renewables contracts commonly incorporate contractual standards of performance that the project must achieve, failing which the owner may levy performance shortfall liquidated damages, reduce the contract price payable, or even reject the project outright. These contractual warranties often require the plant to achieve a specified average megawatt-hour output under typical weather conditions. It is important that the contract is sufficiently clear as to how the plant's performance is to be measured for this purpose, over what period, and what adjustments can be made to the output to account for factors like changes in the weather, losses resulting from O&M and unplanned operational outages, so as to avoid disputes over whether the performance standards have been met.

Similarly, clearly well-defined performance standards can be highly effective in avoiding disputes over the quality of performance. Express reference to the particular codes and standards to which equipment must be certified, or with which a contractor must comply when designing and constructing the plant, can avoid later disputes over whether a contractor's performance was adequate. For example, expressly stating that the American Society of Mechanical Engineering standards are mandatory can avoid an argument that compliance with some other standard is sufficient. Conversely, vaguely worded standards can cause confusion, particularly given the continuously evolving technological benchmarks in the renewables sector. For example, a warranty that a plant will adopt 'state of the art' technology gives rise to a host of questions: Does this mean the latest cutting edge technology, or whatever is readily available on the market? And at what point is the standard to be determined – when the contract is signed, when the design is developed, or when the plant is actually constructed? There can be – and often is – a time lag between each of those stages.

It may also be prudent to include in the contract an agreed list of approved subcontractors the owner considers suitable (and in respect of which the owner has done thorough due diligence), to avoid later arguments concerning the suitability of a contractor's choice of subcontractor and whether that subcontractor had sufficient relevant experience.

price review or adjustment clause can be a relatively straightforward way to adjust the contract price where geopolitical factors lead to increased prices. Such a clause allows for the contract price to be adjusted to reflect changes in the market. Clarity as to when the obligation to renegotiate arises and how the contract price is to be adjusted is key. It is also important to think about governing law in this context. Certain civil laws codify the concept of hardship or extreme difficulty, allowing the parties to adapt, renegotiate or even terminate a contract where there are unexpected circumstances (such as extreme, unforeseen price inflation impacting a party's ability to perform) without the need for such a provision to be written into the contract.

4.7 Variations, extensions of time and extra cost

Contracts for the delivery of a renewables project typically include clauses setting out the circumstances in which one party can claim additional time and cost, the categories of cost that are recoverable and the procedure to follow to submit a claim. Where these clauses are very clearly worded, they can help mitigate disputes risk. Parties should pay particular attention to the notice requirements in such clauses, as failure to adhere to contractual notice stipulations can result in parties losing their right to pursue a claim entirely. Parties to English law-governed contracts should also be aware that where a construction contract confers a discretion on one party (such as to allow or refuse a variation claim), there can be a term implied requiring that discretion is exercised honestly and in good faith.

4.8 *Force majeure* clauses

Force majeure clauses are contractual provisions providing for the suspension or variation of performance obligations in certain circumstances beyond the parties' control, such as war, natural disaster or pandemic. In a common law context, *force majeure* is not a standalone legal doctrine – whether it exists and applies to excuse one party's failure to perform a contract depends on the particular words of the *force majeure* clause included in that contract. It is therefore crucial that such clauses are unambiguous and closely followed by the party seeking to rely on them. The clause might list criteria that must be met in order for an event to qualify as *force majeure*, or list the specific circumstances in which the clause will operate. The inclusion of such a clause can be particularly beneficial in a renewables context given the vulnerability of such projects to unpredictable weather conditions and supply chain disruption.

Particular attention must be paid to any contractual requirements regarding notice – whether or not notice requirements act as preconditions to relief from performance is a common area of dispute that is readily avoidable with careful drafting. Where the contract is governed by common law and there is a desire to have the ability to reopen the parties' original contractual bargain on the basis of hardship, an express hardship clause should also be included. And parties operating in civil law jurisdictions should beware that civil law concepts such as hardship and *force majeure* as a legal doctrine might arguably apply on a mandatory basis, that is, they cannot be excluded by the parties through the choice of English or another common law, which has no legal concept of hardship, as the governing law.

4.9 Defect rectification clauses

Given the relatively high risk of technology failures in renewables projects using new and innovative technologies, contracts typically include defect rectification obligations, which require a contractor to return to site to repair or replace any defective equipment. It is important that such clauses make clear when a contractor will be so obliged, as well as when the employer can step in to remedy a defect itself (should, for example, the contractor fail to rectify the defective works). Defect rectification clauses should also clarify what form that rectification might take and how and when the employer can recover its costs from the contractor. The contractor will want certainty as to when its obligations under such clauses will cease to apply.

Like many construction contracts, renewables contracts often include limitation or exclusion of liability clauses. Such clauses serve to limit or cap a company's potential liability.

4.10 Limitation of liability clauses

Like many construction contracts, renewables contracts often include limitation or exclusion of liability clauses. Such clauses serve to limit or cap a company's potential liability. Again, it is important that such clauses are sufficiently clearly drafted (especially where formulae are used to calculate the cap) so that it is clear, for example, whether or not a cap applies to individual claims or in aggregate to all potential claims under the contract.[89]

4.11 Dispute resolution provisions

Finally, a well-structured dispute resolution provision can mitigate the risk of formal proceedings being commenced, by requiring parties to meet and attempt to resolve a dispute amicably, or to wait for a number of weeks or months after sending a notice of dispute before commencing court or arbitration proceedings. Such clauses can result in an early settlement; but query whether, where there is a realistic prospect of settlement, parties need a contractual mechanism compelling them to pursue formal mediation (or other settlement) proceedings to resolve their dispute. Ultimately, the dispute resolution provision will ensure that the parties have a means of avoiding a deadlock and resolving disputes that might otherwise prevent conclusion of the project. As discussed further in Chapter V, careful drafting is important to make sure any such clause (especially a tiered dispute resolution clause) is enforceable and cannot be tactically misused by a party to delay or disrupt the meaningful resolution of a dispute.

Despite there being various means of mitigating disputes risk, differences are sometimes inevitable. Where disputes do arise, the mix of technical factual issues, the potential mix of applicable laws and the broad range of expert and factual evidence that may be needed, all point towards the inherent flexibility of international arbitration which, when compared with domestic litigation processes, offers significant advantages, as discussed in the following chapters.

IV. International arbitration

International arbitration has long been the mechanism of choice for international energy and construction dispute resolution.[90] The prevalence of arbitration in these sectors is clear from the statistics of some of the major arbitral institutions, which record a high proportion of both energy- and construction-related cases each year.[91] Arbitration is also the dispute resolution mechanism specified in most BITs and MITs, including the ECT. In this chapter, we explain what arbitration is, and why its key features make it an attractive mechanism for resolving renewables disputes. Indeed, several of the main arbitral institutions have reported an increase in renewable energy issues in the cases they administer.[92]

1. What is international arbitration?

Arbitration is a private, consensual and binding dispute resolution process, whereby two or more parties agree to submit their dispute to a tribunal specifically constituted for the purpose of making a final and binding decision (known as an 'award'). Arbitration is distinct from court litigation and has long been used as a method for resolving international disputes,[93] tracing its roots at least as far back as the trade guilds of medieval Europe (although some legal historians have suggested a similar process was known to the ancient Egyptians).

Arbitration is a party-controlled process: among other things, the

Disputes in the renewables sector often require a final and binding determination to be made (for example, as to whether contractual guarantees have been met, who is responsible for rectifying key equipment, or how a clause providing for O&M payments is to be interpreted) to allow the project to continue with certainty to completion, or for the remainder of its operational life.

parties stipulate the manner in which the arbitration proceeds, the law that governs it, where it takes place, the procedural rules, and the identity of the arbitrator(s) who will decide the dispute. Arbitration is only available where the parties have agreed to it, either in the dispute resolution clause in their contract or in a separate submission agreement signed after a dispute has arisen (although the latter is relatively uncommon).

We set out in the following sections the key characteristics of commercial arbitration (as distinct from investor–state arbitration) which make it a particularly attractive process for the resolution of disputes in the renewables sector.

2. A final and binding decision

Disputes in the renewables sector often require a final and binding determination to be made (for example, as to whether contractual guarantees have been met, who is responsible for rectifying key equipment, or how a clause providing for O&M payments is to be interpreted) to allow the project to continue with certainty to completion, or for the remainder of its operational life. Years of appeals from one court to another do little for certainty and stability. Arbitration allows for finality. The parties' ability to appeal or challenge an arbitral award is much more limited than is the case with court judgments. The extent to which an arbitral award can be challenged is a question for the law of the 'seat' of the arbitration (the seat is discussed further in Chapter V) and is generally heavily circumscribed, commonly limited to situations where something has gone seriously awry in the process.

As at July 2024, legislation based on the UNCITRAL Model Law on International Commercial Arbitration ('the Model Law') has been adopted in 126 jurisdictions.[94] The Model Law reflects worldwide consensus on key aspects of international arbitration. Under Article 34 of the 2006 edition of the Model Law, an application for setting aside is the exclusive recourse against an arbitral award. An award may only be set aside on very limited grounds, including where:

- a party was under some incapacity or the arbitration agreement was invalid;
- a party was not given proper notice of the proceedings or was otherwise unable to present its case;
- the award deals with matters beyond the scope of the submission to arbitration;
- the composition of the tribunal or the arbitral procedure was not in accordance with the parties' agreement;
- the subject matter of the dispute is not capable of settlement by arbitration under the law of the seat of arbitration; or
- the award is in conflict with the public policy of the seat.

In England and Wales, the Arbitration Act 1996 sets out only three grounds on which an arbitral award can be challenged; that is:

- where the tribunal lacked jurisdiction to resolve the dispute (provided that a party made an objection on this basis at an early stage in the proceedings);[95]
- where there is a serious irregularity affecting the tribunal, the proceedings or the award (for example, the award has been obtained by fraud, or the tribunal has exceeded its powers);[96] or
- on a question of law arising out the award[97] (although this is almost always excluded where institutional arbitral rules have been adopted).

The UK government recently published an Arbitration Bill which includes an additional rule prohibiting a party from raising a new objection or presenting new evidence to a court in support of a challenge unless it can demonstrate that it could not have put that evidence before the arbitral tribunal.[98]

A party seeking to challenge an award must bring the application within 28 days, having first complied with any available internal process of appeal or review and any recourse for the correction of the award or issuance of an additional award.[99] It is clear from these requirements that, as a matter of English law, the ability to challenge an award on a point of law is very limited (and much more strictly curtailed than the ability to appeal an English court judgment).

It should be clear that the chances of overturning an award are very slim indeed. While the certainty this provides may often be attractive, it is something of a double-edged sword for the unsuccessful party!

3. A decision enforceable outside the parties' home jurisdictions

In reality, awards are generally complied with,[100] but where enforcement is necessary, arbitration has a unique advantage in comparison with litigation in the shape of the United Nations Convention on the Recognition and Enforcement of Foreign Arbitral Awards, signed in New York in 1958 ('the New York Convention'), which provides for the recognition and enforcement of arbitral awards in the local courts of the contracting parties.[101] As at July 2024, there were 172 state parties to the New York Convention,[102] and it is supplemented by a number of regional arbitration conventions.[103] The New York Convention requires contracting states to recognise arbitration agreements in writing as valid and to refer parties who have entered into an arbitration agreement to arbitration should they seek to commence court proceedings, unless the arbitration agreement is "null and void, inoperative or incapable of being performed".[104] Importantly, it also requires contracting states to recognise[105] foreign arbitration awards as binding and to enforce[106] them as though they were awards made in that state.[107]

There are particular circumstances in which a national court in a contracting state to the New York Convention may refuse to recognise and enforce an award. These are set out in Article V of the Convention, and it is notable that none provide for a review of the merits of the substantive decision.[108]

The effect of the New York Convention is that it is often easier to enforce an arbitral award outside the place where the arbitration took place, or where the parties are based, than may be the case with a court judgment. While there are some regional enforcement regimes that apply to allow the enforcement of foreign court judgments,[109] there is no equivalent to the New York Convention in terms of the number of signatory states.[110] Instead, the enforceability of a foreign court judgment will likely turn on any reciprocal enforcement treaty between the country where the judgment is made and the country where enforcement is sought. The ease of global enforceability is consistently cited as one of the most significant benefits of international arbitration,[111] and it is a particularly important feature for projects in the renewables sector, given the potential involvement of

The effect of the New York Convention is that it is often easier to enforce an arbitral award outside the place where the arbitration took place, or where the parties are based, than may be the case with a court judgment.

parties from multiple jurisdictions and the likely need to seek enforcement in a foreign jurisdiction where a counterparty holds assets.

4. Arbitration is perceived as a more neutral forum for disputes involving parties from multiple jurisdictions

Arbitration allows parties to choose a neutral place (and accordingly a neutral procedural law) where their disputes will be heard and determined, thereby avoiding complex jurisdictional disputes. Where two parties are from different jurisdictions, this avoids one party having to submit to the jurisdiction of the courts in the home state of the other party. This may be particularly beneficial in renewables projects located in emerging and developing economies, where there might be a perceived risk that litigation before the local courts in that country could result in delay or, at worst, bias or corruption in favour of the local counterparty (which could be a state-owned entity).

5. Appointing arbitrators with relevant expertise

The relatively new technology used in renewables projects means that disputes will more often than not involve complex technical issues. Arbitration provides the parties with significant control over the constitution of the arbitral tribunal that will determine their dispute. Unlike litigation, where the dispute is heard by a judge appointed in accordance with the court's roster, arbitration allows parties to choose their arbitrators. Parties can therefore choose decision makers with relevant expertise or experience to ensure the fairest outcome. The ability to control who determines a dispute is one of arbitration's most valuable features – 60% of respondents to a survey conducted by the School of International Arbitration at Queen Mary University of London (QMUL) in 2022 identified the ability to choose arbitrators with relevant technical expertise to be arbitration's most important feature in the context of resolving energy disputes.[112]

There is no obligation on the parties to appoint as arbitrators legally qualified and trained professionals (although they generally do) – parties are free to appoint anyone who has experience relevant to the dispute. It might be appropriate, for example, to appoint an engineer in a delay dispute, or an architect in a dispute involving issues of design. QMUL's 2019 international arbitration survey identified that 38% of respondents had experience of technical experts being appointed to an arbitral panel.[113] The PCA's Optional Rules for Arbitration of Disputes Relating to Natural Resources and/or the Environment provide for the creation of a specialised list of arbitrators with expertise in environmental issues who can be called upon in environmental disputes.[114]

6. Flexibility of process

Unlike litigation, where the procedure is heavily circumscribed and often set out in legislation, arbitral procedure is firmly in the parties' hands. The flexibility of arbitration allows parties to think outside the box in deploying the various procedural tools at their disposal to tailor the arbitration process to their particular dispute. Most arbitral rules impose a duty on the tribunal to adopt a procedure that promotes efficiency and avoids delay and expense, and grant the tribunal a wide discretion to make orders to discharge those duties (subject to any applicable law).[115] Some of the procedural tools offered by arbitration that in our experience can be most effective are discussed further in Chapter VI.

7. Privacy and confidentiality

Parties to an arbitration can, and often do, agree to keep the very fact of the arbitration – and all documents created or exchanged – confidential, and arbitration hearings are generally conducted in private. Some arbitral rules and curial laws contain express provisions for private hearings and the confidentiality of the arbitration.[116] These considerations are important for disputes in the renewables sector, where the technology deployed might be highly confidential, contracts might include sensitive pricing information, and companies branching out into new industries will be keen to avoid any reputational harm that may follow should they be reported as being involved in a dispute. This is a significant benefit of arbitration – by contrast, court hearings and judgments, and documents filed in those proceedings are, in many jurisdictions, accessible to the general public.

Parties that are concerned to keep any arbitration proceedings confidential should first consider what provisions for confidentiality form part of the applicable procedural or governing law and arbitration rules and their contractual documentation. Where those provisions are not adequate, the parties can agree to additional confidentiality requirements, either by incorporating appropriate wording into their arbitration agreement (as explained further in Chapter V), or by agreeing to confidentiality provisions in the terms of reference or procedural order governing their proceedings once arbitration has been commenced.

8. The choice of forum is clear

The involvement of multiple international parties in a renewables project means that it is possible that multiple laws might apply in the event of a dispute, including:

- the law of the place where the project is implemented;
- the law of the place where key pieces of equipment are manufactured; and
- the respective laws of the home states of the parties involved.

In the absence of a clear choice by the parties of the forum in which these disputes should be resolved, there may be lengthy and complicated proceedings, or even multiple concurrent proceedings in several courts, to determine which national court has jurisdiction to hear the dispute. A clearly drafted and enforceable arbitration agreement excludes the jurisdiction of all courts in favour of arbitration, thus removing the risk of multiple proceedings to determine the court of competent jurisdiction.

9. Types of relief available in arbitration proceedings

Arbitral tribunals are empowered by the parties to grant relief and generally have the power to order declaratory relief and award damages. Virtually all institutional rules give tribunals the power to grant any interim relief that they deem appropriate in the circumstances,[117] and allow parties the option of obtaining relief from a court.[118] The ICC Rules, for example, allow an arbitral tribunal to "order any interim or conservatory measure it deems appropriate",[119] and the PCA's Environmental Rules expressly grant a tribunal the power to take any interim measures that it deems necessary to prevent serious harm to the environment or the marine environment falling within the subject matter of the dispute.[120] As discussed further in Chapter V, most arbitral rules now also provide for emergency arbitration and expedited tribunal formation in certain circumstances. Parties might seek to use these mechanisms to restrain a party from taking steps to dispose of equipment or materials that might be needed as evidence in the arbitration proceedings, or in relation to a threatened call upon a performance bond, for example. In some instances, emergency or expedited arbitration procedures might not be fast enough. In those circumstances, many arbitral laws allow the parties to approach the courts of the seat for interim relief in support of the arbitration, pending constitution of the tribunal.

V. Getting the basics right: drafting an effective arbitration agreement

The arbitration agreement is normally located in the dispute resolution provisions within the parties' main contract and is normally referred to as an 'arbitration clause'. Getting the drafting of the arbitration clause right is critical to avoiding lengthy and costly satellite disputes about the meaning and scope of the clause. Giving early consideration to the particular transaction and the types of disputes that might arise, and accounting for those factors in the arbitration clause itself, can save significant costs and time in the long run. In this chapter, we draw together some of the lessons learned from arbitrating renewables disputes and highlight the key considerations for drafting an effective arbitration clause.

1. The scope of the clause

It is of fundamental importance that the clause is clear in its reference to arbitration so that there is no uncertainty as to the appropriate forum for the resolution of disputes or the jurisdiction of the arbitral tribunal. The arbitration clause should clearly identify which disputes must be referred to arbitration and which, if any, are outside the scope of the arbitration agreement. It is generally preferable to have all disputes referred to arbitration so as to avoid satellite disputes about what is and is not included in the arbitration agreement. A common approach is to adopt a broadly worded clause that refers to arbitration 'any dispute or difference' arising 'out of, under or in connection with'

Getting the drafting of the arbitration clause right is critical to avoiding lengthy and costly satellite disputes about the meaning and scope of the clause.

a contract. Internationally, arbitration agreements are generally interpreted expansively, in line with the pro-arbitration presumption that parties intend their arbitration agreement to encompass all disputes arising out of their relationship and to avoid sending disputes to multiple different forums.[121]

2. Multi-tiered arbitration clauses

Given the importance of preserving contractual relationships for the duration of the project's operational lifetime and the significant time and costs involved in arbitration, it is not unusual for renewables contracts to have multi-tiered dispute resolution clauses that require parties to engage in a series of increasingly formal steps to attempt to resolve any dispute before commencing arbitration. These clauses also commonly require the sending of a notice of dispute describing exactly what a party intends to refer to arbitration.

Three-tiered dispute resolution clause

The first tier of a dispute resolution clause will generally be an attempt at amicable settlement by the parties for a number of weeks or months, or a structured negotiation at senior management level. A mandatory cooling-off period can allow parties to weigh up the merits of the dispute and the risk and expense of pursuing formal proceedings, and might make them more amenable to settlement.

The next tier in a multi-tiered clause might be a more structured process involving a neutral third party with relevant expertise, such as compulsory mediation, where the neutral party encourages negotiation and compromise, or expert determination, where an expert makes a decision on the merits. Dispute resolution clauses in construction and infrastructure project contracts often require reference to a dispute board, which is a panel of experts that is either standing (established at the beginning of the project) or *ad hoc* (brought into existence as and when required).[122] The extent to which the finding of any expert or dispute board is binding will depend on the parties' agreement. However, it is common that both a party's failure to comply with a binding expert determination and its ability to challenge a non-binding determination are both disputes that can be referred to arbitration. For example, FIDIC's *Silver Book*, which is a standard form of contract for the construction of a power plant on a turnkey basis,[123] requires disputes to be referred to a standing dispute avoidance and adjudication board before they are referred to arbitration under the ICC Rules.[124]

The final tier in a multi-tiered dispute resolution clause would be reference to arbitration.

While such clauses are often included in a contract with the intention of avoiding the need to resort to formal legal proceedings, they should be treated with caution. If they are not followed exactly, they can result in an arbitration tribunal not having jurisdiction over a dispute, a claim being inadmissible, or the arbitration proceedings being stayed until all steps in the clause have been carried out. In our experience, the party on the receiving end of a notice of arbitration will more often than not scrutinise a multi-tiered dispute resolution clause for possible arguments that the clause has not been complied with, in an attempt to delay substantive commencement of the proceedings (or to frustrate those proceedings entirely).

Whether or not pre-arbitration steps are mandatory is not straightforward and differs from jurisdiction to jurisdiction. As a matter of English law, multi-tiered dispute resolution clauses are generally enforceable provided they are:

- certain as to exactly what is required and the consequences of non-compliance;
- expressed in sufficiently mandatory language (such as use of the word 'shall'); and
- not contrary to public policy or to any specific legislation.[125]

As a matter of English law, failure to comply with any mandatory pre-arbitration steps can render a claim inadmissible.[126] Mandatory preconditions to the commencement of an arbitration should therefore only be drafted where that is very clearly the parties' considered intention; otherwise, they may serve to open the door to litigation in domestic courts, which the parties may have been keen to avoid.

It is important that parties review such clauses and make sure all the steps – in particular any time limits and notice requirements – have been followed before commencing arbitration proceedings, to ensure efficient resolution of the dispute.

3. The seat of the arbitration

Parties to an arbitration are free to determine a neutral seat, or legal place, for their dispute to be heard that bears no connection to any of the parties or their home states – the neutrality this offers will often be very attractive, as it prevents either party from gaining an advantage based on their own jurisdiction. The seat of the arbitration is an important part of any arbitration agreement as it dictates:

- which courts will have supervisory jurisdiction over the arbitration, including adjudicating applications related to it. The seat also establishes the extent of court intervention in the

Parties may opt either for institutional arbitration, administered by an arbitral institution in accordance with its rules, or ad hoc *arbitration, which is not administered by an institution and may or may not follow any prescribed arbitral rules.*

arbitration process. It is important to consider the reputation of the courts of the chosen seat for probity, as well as a favourable attitude to arbitration. Popular seats include England, Singapore, France, Switzerland and Sweden, because they have modern arbitration regimes, either directly incorporating the Model Law or being substantially similar. QMUL's 2022 Survey identified London and Singapore as the most popular seats for resolving energy-related disputes, closely followed by Paris;[127]

- the procedural law governing the arbitration. The procedural law of the arbitration typically sets out the minimum procedural requirements that the arbitration must follow and the grounds on which an award may be challenged or enforced. For example, an arbitration seated in London will be subject to the Arbitration Act 1996;
- whether the dispute is arbitrable in that country, or is something over which the local courts reserve jurisdiction; and
- the enforceability of the award, as the seat of the arbitration determines the 'nationality' of the award, including for the purposes of the New York Convention.

Given the international nature of most renewables projects, and the reciprocity reservation made by some signatories,[128] it is important that the chosen seat has ratified the New York Convention.[129]

4. The procedural rules that will apply

Parties may opt either for institutional arbitration, administered by an arbitral institution in accordance with its rules, or *ad hoc* arbitration, which is not administered by an institution and may or may not follow any prescribed arbitral rules.

4.1 Institutional arbitration

An institutional arbitration is one where the arbitration is administered and supervised by an arbitral institution, typically in accordance with that institution's rules. The arbitral institution will appoint the tribunal, determine the tribunal's fees and oversee various administrative matters. Some institutions (such as the ICC and the Singapore International Arbitration Centre (SIAC)) also scrutinise draft awards to make sure there are no readily apparent enforceability concerns. Institutional arbitration is generally favoured over *ad hoc* arbitration because institutions can step in when a party fails or refuses to cooperate.

There are a number of established arbitral institutions to which parties may refer their disputes. According to QMUL's 2019 arbitration survey, the most preferred arbitral institutions selected in the construction sector are the ICC and the London Court of International Arbitration (LCIA).[130] The ICC is particularly popular in the energy, construction and engineering sectors, which regularly make up the largest proportion of its case load.[131] How arbitrators' fees and administrative fees are calculated differs between institutions, and can influence the parties' choice of institutional rules, with some institutions (such as the ICC, SIAC and SCC) calculating fees by reference to the amount in dispute and others (such as the LCIA) calculating fees at capped hourly rates based on time spent by the tribunal.

Key considerations in selecting an institution are:

- its international reputation;
- its responsiveness;
- its fees and flexibility; and
- whether the parties might wish to adopt an expedited procedure or apply for summary dismissal of a manifestly unmeritorious claim (as explained in section 11 below).

While a careful reading of the rules can assist, input from legal counsel with experience of arbitrating under the institutional rules is invaluable in terms of informing the parties as to how the institution in question might handle the proceedings, and how particular nuances in the rules might benefit or prejudice one party or the other.

Legal counsel can also advise on whether there are any specific requirements that must be met in order to access a particular institution. For example, parties to contracts with a state or state-owned entity that might have commercial claims in the future should be aware that Article 25 of the ICSID Convention sets out particular criteria that must be met for parties to access the arbitration facilities provided by ICSID under the ICSID Convention.[132] Broadly, in order for a tribunal constituted under the ICSID Convention to have jurisdiction, the dispute in issue must be between a contracting state party to the Convention and a national from another contracting state party. Additionally, the dispute must arise directly out of an 'investment' (which term is not exhaustively defined in the Convention). Particular issues arise with respect to state-owned entities which must be 'designated' to ICSID by the contracting state in order for an ICSID tribunal to have jurisdiction over that entity. It may be possible to satisfy these jurisdictional requirements through the arbitration agreement itself and so it is important for parties contracting with a state (or a state-owned entity) who are considering ICSID as an arbitration institution to seek specialist legal advice.

4.2 *Ad hoc* arbitration

An *ad hoc* arbitration is not administered by an arbitral institution but can be conducted either on the basis of rules prepared from scratch by the parties or existing *ad hoc* arbitration rules, such as the UNCITRAL Rules. *Ad hoc* arbitration is entirely managed by the parties, who are responsible for matters such as the appointment of the tribunal, arranging the logistics of the hearing, and negotiating directly with the arbitrator in respect of their fees. The potential benefit of *ad hoc* arbitration is that it may be quicker and more flexible than institutional arbitration – but it may also cause problems where parties refuse to cooperate or seek to delay the proceedings, including by failing to nominate an arbitrator, in which case parties will be bound by the procedural law of the arbitration. *Ad hoc* arbitration is generally favoured in sectors that are familiar with arbitration, such as the shipping sector. Outside areas where it is established, it is seldom a good idea and can all too easily lead to arguments about process that end up being referred for resolution to the court of the seat.

5. The tribunal

The arbitration agreement should specify the number of arbitrators, how they will be appointed and any particular requirements (such as nationality or expertise) that the parties have agreed the arbitrators should have. The number of arbitrators is usually one or three (never an even number), and if not specified in the arbitration agreement the relevant rules will generally contain a default position. While a sole arbitrator is usually less expensive than a panel of three, in large-scale projects it is more common to have a three-person arbitration tribunal, with one arbitrator nominated by each party and a third 'neutral' presiding or chair arbitrator. Most arbitration agreements will allow for the presiding arbitrator to be chosen by the party-nominated arbitrators (with or without reference to the parties). In renewables projects, it might be sensible for the parties to agree to a set of characteristics they would like the presiding arbitrator to possess. For example, the parties might agree that it is important that they have previous experience of disputes involving a similar contractual structure to their project, and write this requirement into their arbitration agreement (or, at the very least, require in the arbitration agreement that the party-nominated arbitrators consult with the parties prior to appointing a chairperson). It is important that any requirements are carefully worded – too much specificity could lead to the arbitration clause being unworkable because no qualified individual can be found. It is advisable to set a deadline for the appointment of arbitrators to avoid delays caused by a party's refusal to cooperate. If the deadline is not met, the appointment could be referred to the institution or, in the case of *ad hoc* proceedings, an independent appointing authority.

6. The choice of law governing the contract

The international nature of renewables projects means that it is a common feature of contracts in the sector to specify a neutral governing law. The governing law is the substantive law used to

If the law governing the arbitration agreement is not specified, there is a risk of a satellite dispute, or potentially concurrent disputes, to determine which law applies, particularly where the governing law of the main contract does not align with the seat of the arbitration.

adjudicate the parties' obligations. A key factor in selecting the governing law is its certainty when applied to commercial contracts. English law is a popular choice for that reason. Where the governing law of the contract is not specified, the tribunal will choose, generally by reference to the choice of law rules in the seat of the arbitration.

When selecting a governing law, parties should be aware that the chosen law will not necessarily rule out the application of another law in the event of a dispute. The local law at the place of performance will likely apply in addressing corporate issues attaching to the SPV and issues of property and employment; it might also govern any tortious claims. There is also scope for local law at the place of performance to apply on the basis of principles of mandatory application of laws. This can come as something of a surprise to unprepared parties. Using international arbitration to resolve disputes can ensure that the relevant decision makers are appropriately qualified in all applicable laws or, at the very least, that there is scope to adduce foreign law expert evidence to inform the tribunal on laws in which they are not qualified.

7. The law of the arbitration agreement

Separately, it is advisable to specify within the arbitration clause the law governing the arbitration agreement itself. This is because the arbitration agreement is a contract in its own right, separate from the broader contract in which it resides (this is known as the principle of separability).[133] The law of the arbitration agreement determines its interpretation and application, and would therefore be used to determine whether any dispute falls within its scope. If the law governing the arbitration agreement is not specified, there is a risk of a satellite dispute, or potentially concurrent disputes, to determine which law applies, particularly where the governing law of the main contract does not align with the seat of the arbitration. The United Kingdom's Arbitration Bill stipulates that the governing law of the arbitration agreement will be the law of the seat of the arbitration unless the parties expressly agree otherwise.[134] It is nevertheless sensible to state expressly which law governs the arbitration agreement, and ideally to make sure it aligns with the chosen seat.

8. Civil law vs common law

When selecting a neutral governing law, parties generally have a choice between a common law (such as English, Australian, Canadian, Singaporean or United States law) and a civil law (such as French, German or Spanish law). This choice is important; it will impact how the contract is interpreted, whether the parties must perform their obligations in good faith, the extent to which concepts such as *force majeure* or hardship might excuse a failure to perform the contract, and what remedies are available in the event of a breach.

Under English law (and most common law systems) the interpretation of a contract is an objective exercise that focuses on the natural and ordinary meaning of the words used by the parties. Where there is more than one possible construction, the court or tribunal can prefer the construction that is consistent with business common sense.

Civil law systems, on the other hand, adopt a subjective test that focuses on establishing what the parties intended rather than the actual words used. Civil law systems often imply a duty of good faith in contracts, particularly in relation to negotiations. Common law systems will generally not impose a general obligation of good faith – if the parties want to be bound by such an obligation they must state so expressly in their contract (noting, however, that an obligation to negotiate in good faith may constitute an agreement to agree, which would generally be unenforceable, at least under English law).

Similarly, under most common law systems (including English law) there is no generally applicable hardship or *force majeure* doctrine. If the parties wish to make use of such mechanisms they must be written into the contract and the scope and effect of any *force majeure* event will be a matter of construction of the clause. On the other hand, the doctrines of *force majeure* and hardship are recognised in many civil law codes. These doctrines might operate to excuse contractual non-performance, and can ultimately result in termination of the contract or adjustment of its terms.

The choice between civil or common law will impact the parties' ability to terminate a contract in the event of a repudiatory breach, the enforceability of a liquidated damages provision and the recoverability of certain categories of loss.

Being alive to the different ways in which a contract might fall to be performed depending on the choice of law is crucial to avoid surprise, both during contractual performance and in the event of a dispute.

9. Provision for joinder and consolidation

The complex and multi-party nature of a renewables project means that it is possible that a dispute will involve several contracts between several parties. As arbitration is a consensual process, the jurisdiction of an arbitral tribunal arises only from the parties' agreement to arbitrate. Save where joinder or consolidation is possible, the tribunal will not have jurisdiction over any potentially interested or affected third parties or related disputes. The parties may find it preferable to have multiple disputes resolved in a single consolidated arbitration.

The prospects of successfully consolidating multiple arbitrations under several agreements would be significantly improved if each contract contained an identical arbitration clause. Alternatively, all the parties might enter into a separate umbrella arbitration agreement that provides for a single arbitration to be commenced in respect of disputes that arise out of multiple contracts.

A number of arbitration rules provide for the joinder of third parties and the consolidation of multiple disputes (such as the Hong Kong International Arbitration Centre (HKIAC) Rules, the ICC Rules, the LCIA Rules, the SCC Rules, the SIAC Rules, the UNCITRAL Rules, the Australian Centre for International Commercial Arbitration (ACICA) Rules, the Dubai International Centre for Arbitration (DCIA) Rules and the Swiss Chambers' Arbitration Institution (SCAI) Rules ('The Swiss Rules')).[135] Certain rules allow a claimant to serve a composite request for arbitration in order to commence multiple arbitrations under more than one arbitration agreement.[136] Institutional rules might also give the tribunal the power to order that two or more arbitrations be run concurrently where the same tribunal is appointed to multiple arbitrations under compatible arbitration agreements or between the same parties.[137] There may be differences in the institutional rules as to the circumstances in which a third party can be joined to an arbitration or multiple arbitrations can be consolidated. It is therefore important to engage with counsel when drafting the contract to ensure the appropriate institutional rules are agreed upon.

However, in our experience, even express provision for joinder or consolidation in the applicable rules does not necessarily guarantee that it will be possible. Under certain rules, joinder applications will be granted almost automatically where there is an arbitration agreement that binds the third party, without any real review of the merits of joining such a third party. This may be to a party's benefit, but could also come as a surprise to those proceeding without proper legal advice. It is important to give proper thought, at the outset of a dispute and before commencing proceedings, to whether consolidation is necessary – consolidation applications made too late, particularly once a tribunal has been appointed (should the same tribunal not be appointed to hear the separate dispute), may be unsuccessful.

10. Provision for confidentiality

There is no general rule of confidentiality in arbitration; rather, the level of privacy and confidentiality typically depends on any agreed contractual provisions and the seat of the arbitration (as national rules diverge on the issue). Some institutions provide for confidentiality as a default rule. For example, the LCIA Rules require the parties to keep confidential all awards in the arbitration and any materials created for the purposes of the arbitration, as well as all other documents produced by another party not otherwise in the public domain (save

Even where confidentiality clauses are contained in the main contract, they might not clearly cover the arbitration proceedings themselves. This can give rise to disputes, and so it is better to be clear in the arbitration agreement itself or, if that has not happened, then in the first procedural order produced in the arbitration.

where disclosure may be required by a legal duty, to protect or pursue a legal right, or to enforce or challenge an award).[138] However, where confidentiality is an important consideration, this should be expressly provided for in the arbitration agreement. Even where confidentiality clauses are contained in the main contract, they might not clearly cover the arbitration proceedings themselves. This can give rise to disputes, and so it is better to be clear in the arbitration agreement itself or, if that has not happened, then in the first procedural order produced in the arbitration (discussed further in Chapter VI).

11. The need for a quick resolution

It is often critical that disputes arising in the course of a renewables project are resolved quickly. Both the technology involved and the applicable regulatory framework are vulnerable to change, and so it is not always possible to wait for years for a resolution. Parties who anticipate that a dispute may need to be resolved quickly may want to consider incorporating into their arbitration clause the rules of an institution that will facilitate emergency or expedited proceedings.

11.1 Emergency arbitration

The arbitration rules of a number of arbitral institutions – including the ACICA,[139] the DIAC,[140] the HKIAC,[141] the ICC,[142] the LCIA,[143] the SCC,[144] the SIAC[145] and the Swiss Rules[146] – provide for the appointment of an emergency arbitrator to conduct emergency proceedings pending formation of the tribunal. The timeframe for an emergency arbitrator to make its decision varies between rules, but is generally between five and 15 days following appointment.[147] Orders made by the emergency arbitrator are generally not binding on the tribunal once it has been constituted.[148] Emergency arbitration is a useful tool when urgent interim relief is required that cannot await the constitution of the tribunal; for example, where an injunction is sought to prevent a call on a performance bond.

11.2 Expedited proceedings

The rules of certain arbitral institutions also provide for disputes under a certain value to be determined on an expedited basis before a sole arbitrator. Expedited arbitration provisions allow for the swift appointment of the tribunal, and for the procedure to be carried out on an accelerated timetable. For example:

- The SCC offers an expedited arbitration procedure that is available by consent and provides for a final award within three months of the date the case was referred to the tribunal.[149]
- The ICC offers an expedited procedure that automatically applies where the aggregate amount in dispute is below a certain threshold (US$3 million for arbitration agreements entered into after 1 January 2021),[150] unless the parties opt out or the ICC Court of Arbitration considers it inappropriate.[151] The parties can also opt into the expedited procedure at any time. The procedure:
    - cuts out the terms of reference stage;
    - requires a case management conference within 15 days of the date on which the file was transmitted to the tribunal;
    - provides that the arbitral tribunal may make its award on the basis of documents only; and
    - may limit the number, length and scope of written submissions and witness evidence.

  The final award is expected to be rendered within six months of the case management conference.
- The SIAC Rules contain an expedited procedure that provides for a complete arbitration to take place within six months of formation of the arbitral tribunal. The procedure is available by consent, when the aggregate amount in dispute (ie, the total amount of the claim, any counterclaim, set-off defence or cross-claim) does not exceed SG$6 million, or in cases of exceptional urgency.[152]

These procedures have proven popular. The ICC's 2023 Dispute Resolution Statistics noted that there were 189 new cases administered under the expedited procedure provisions in 2023,[153] and that almost 20% of commercial clean energy disputes referred to the SCC between 2014 and 2018 were registered under its Expedited Rules.[154] Even where there is no express fast track procedure, the procedural rules of arbitration are flexible, so the parties can agree to a truncated timetable to reduce the time to an award.[155]

11.3 Summary disposal of unmeritorious claims

A criticism of international arbitration historically has been that it does not allow for blatantly groundless claims to be disposed of quickly. That position has evolved in recent years, and now the rules of a number of arbitral institutions – including the SCC,[156] the ICC,[157] the SIAC,[158] the HKIAC[159] and the LCIA[160] – provide expressly for the summary dismissal of claims that are manifestly without merit or beyond the tribunal's jurisdiction. Even where the rules do not expressly provide for summary disposition of unmeritorious claims, there is a general consensus that an arbitral tribunal does have summary disposal powers. A tribunal could, therefore, dispose of an arbitration without going through the relatively costly parts of the process such as document production, evidence, and the final merits hearing. This may prove effective where a frivolous or vexatious claim has been filed for purely tactical purposes. However, in practice, tribunals are often reluctant to exercise these powers to avoid potential challenges to the award on the grounds of an alleged lack of due process.

VI. Top tips for resolving renewables disputes through arbitration

So how can the unique flexibility of international arbitration be used most advantageously in renewables disputes? Below we set out the key areas for consideration, based on our experience of advising and acting for clients in this area.

1. Selecting the right arbitrator

As noted in the previous chapter, most large-scale renewables disputes will involve a three-person arbitration tribunal, with each party having the ability to choose its own arbitrator. In that context, the finality of arbitral awards means that selecting the right arbitrator is critical – arguably, the most important choice a party will make throughout the process. Giving proper consideration to potential candidates is crucial. Where awards are published (even in redacted form), they can sometimes give parties a feel for how a particular candidate might decide particular issues. However, in the majority of cases the privacy of the arbitral process, and the confidentiality obligations by which the parties and tribunal are often bound, means there is a lack of clarity regarding a candidate's likely performance, particularly in the case of commercial arbitration. There have been calls for the sharing of knowledge among the international arbitration community through the development of an arbitrator database containing insight into how certain individuals would likely decide particular issues.[161] No such database yet exists, however, and word of mouth remains the best source of intelligence. Engaging an international law firm as counsel is particularly helpful in this respect, given the ability for colleagues within a firm to share information across different jurisdictions.

It is also possible to interview potential arbitrator candidates in order to understand their general approach to the arbitrator role – for example, whether they actively read all the materials or wait until the merits hearing; and whether they are independent operators or defer heavily to their co-arbitrators. Interviews can also be a useful way to flush out possible concerns regarding independence or a lack of availability, which might otherwise cause problems down the line.

2. Importance of the first procedural order

The first procedural order in an arbitration (commonly referred to as 'PO1') is a particularly important document: it records the parties' agreement as to how the arbitration will be conducted. Parties will usually work together to develop this document, either producing a first draft for consideration by the tribunal or commenting on a draft prepared by the tribunal. The preparation of PO1 thus presents an opportunity for early engagement between co-counsel, which can provide helpful insight into how the opposition might approach the proceedings more generally. A thorough and unambiguous PO1 can remove the scope for satellite disputes on procedural issues and increase the efficiency of the proceedings. Important considerations when preparing PO1 are set out in the following sub-sections.

2.1 Document production

In common law litigation, a comprehensive disclosure, or 'discovery', exercise is often required. This is the process whereby parties disclose to each other relevant documents that might help or hinder their case. Disclosure has been roundly criticised by many legal commentators as disproportionately expensive for the benefits it produces, but arbitration does offer an advantage over litigation in the sense that the flexibility of the process allows the parties to agree on the extent of document production. Parties can agree to the production of limited categories of documents only, or indeed to dispense entirely with the process if, for example, documents would likely not resolve disputed factual issues, or if all relevant documents will be attached to the pleadings. In any event, document production in international arbitration is often more limited in scope than discovery in common law litigation proceedings. The obligation is typically limited to the production of specifically defined categories of documents which are relevant to issues in dispute and material to their outcome.

The document production stage of an arbitration nevertheless has the potential to be an onerous, lengthy and expensive process given the widespread use of technology for communications and the consequent myriad sources of potentially producible documents. This is particularly the case on large infrastructure projects, and renewables projects in particular, which often involve multiple parties on each side of the dispute and a long timeframe over which the parties have engaged with each other and third parties.

Further challenges can arise where a shell company is used as the project company, because it is often the stakeholders in the project company who hold potentially relevant documents. Unless those stakeholders are also party to the proceedings, it may not be possible for the tribunal, lacking jurisdiction over those stakeholders, to order the production of relevant and material documents.

Parties are well advised to give early consideration to the scope of document production and the extent of the exercise likely to be required. A key consideration will be who holds the relevant documents, whether such entities or individuals are party to the proceedings, and where they are based. Another is that searches may result in swathes of duplicate documents, making the review process more time-consuming or even, if inadequate time has been set aside for the task, impossible. Making provision for how the document production process will be conducted, and over what period, in PO1 is key to avoiding complications.

Parties might seek to adopt protocols to guide the document production phase. It is common for parties to adopt the International Bar Association Rules on the Taking of Evidence in International Arbitration ('the IBA Rules'), which can be particularly helpful in disputes involving parties and lawyers from mixed legal and cultural backgrounds, who traditionally take different approaches to document production. In common law systems, document disclosure and discovery is an extensive process, and often requires parties to produce all documents relevant to an issue in dispute, whether or not they are helpful to a particular party's case. In civil law jurisdictions, each party is generally only required to produce documents upon which it will rely (and in some civil law jurisdictions, the obligation is further limited to documents upon which it will rely and in respect of arguments for which it has the burden of proof). The IBA Rules represent a compromise between the civil and common law systems of evidence. They anticipate both voluntary production in response to requests for categories of relevant and material documents, and tribunal-ordered production. They provide that parties must produce the documents upon which they rely,[162] but may also request a specific document or a "narrow and specific" category of documents which is "relevant to the case and material to its outcome".[163]

Where significant electronic document production is envisaged (as indeed will be the case on most infrastructure projects these days), it is our experience that the Chartered Institute of Arbitrators (CIArb) Protocol for E-Disclosure in International Arbitration can be especially helpful.[164] The protocol is intended to "encourage early consideration of disclosure of documents in electronic form", and to "focus the parties and the Tribunal on e-disclosure issues",[165] and it stipulates that the tribunal must bring questions of e-disclosure to the parties' attention "at the earliest opportunity and in any event no later than the first management conference".[166] The protocol encourages parties to consider what tools and techniques might be deployed to reduce the cost and burden of e-disclosure, including the use of agreed search terms.[167] Engaging with such protocols from the outset, and making proper provision in the procedural timetable for the process of agreeing on search terms, is crucial if unnecessary delay is to be avoided during the document production process.

2.2 Confidentiality

As explained in Chapter V, parties should give early consideration to whether any confidentiality provisions in the contract, the arbitral rules and the curial law offer sufficient protection, particularly where the arbitration involves sensitive pricing information or intellectual property. If there are any gaps in the protection, the parties can write further protections into PO1. If commercially sensitive information may fall to be produced in the proceedings, the parties might, for example, agree to a 'confidentiality bubble' in which only certain individuals (like the legal team and the arbitral tribunal) are permitted to view the relevant documents.

2.3 Case management techniques

More generally, there are a number of case management techniques that can be deployed to narrow the issues in dispute or to reduce the time and costs associated with arbitration, which should be considered when preparing PO1. Some common case management techniques that have proven useful in our experience are:

- the bifurcation of proceedings and the issuance of one or more partial awards (for example, it is common to bifurcate liability and quantum issues);
- identifying issues that can be decided on the basis of documents alone (and not through oral argument);
- identifying issues that can be resolved by agreement and encouraging alternative dispute resolution (ADR) of those issues;[168]
- use of expert conferencing, where experts giving evidence on similar issues are asked to record any areas of agreement, thereby narrowing the issues in dispute (although this needs to

Parties would be advised to give careful consideration to whether their counterparty, its counsel and the tribunal are from a civil or common law background, and how that may inform their conduct of the proceedings.

be balanced against a risk that the more assertive expert dominates the discussion). The CIArb Protocol for the Use of Party-Appointed Expert Witnesses in International Arbitration can also assist in this regard;
- limiting the production of documentary evidence, for example by requiring parties to produce with their submissions the documents on which they rely (as is typical in a 'memorial' pleading),[169] or limiting document production requests to documents or categories of documents that are relevant and material to the issues in dispute;
- summary dismissal of unmeritorious claims;
- requiring the parties to prepare agreed statements of facts or chronologies;
- abridging periods of time;
- making appropriate use of technology, including by conducting hearings remotely;
- capping the page length or time for the parties to make submissions, or restricting the scope of written statements; and
- the use of sanctions on parties failing to conduct the arbitration with diligence.

Some of these techniques will be more familiar, and hence more palatable, to lawyers from some legal traditions more than others.

The technical nature of renewables arbitrations means that the use of party-appointed experts to submit an independent opinion on technical, environmental or economic issues is frequently of fundamental importance, particularly in an environment where much of the technology remains immature.

Parties would be advised to give careful consideration to whether their counterparty, its counsel and the tribunal are from a civil or common law background, and how that may inform their conduct of the proceedings.

3. Educating the tribunal

Following completion of PO1, the next big challenge for a party involved in a renewables arbitration is how best to educate the tribunal about their case. Renewables disputes are more often than not technically complicated, so it is of the utmost importance that the tribunal is properly briefed on the technical aspects of the dispute. Some of the tools that we have found particularly useful in this respect are outlined below.

3.1 Use of experts

The technical nature of renewables arbitrations means that the use of party-appointed experts to submit an independent opinion on technical, environmental or economic issues is frequently of fundamental importance, particularly in an environment where much of the technology remains immature. Arbitration gives parties wide discretion to appoint expert witnesses to give technical evidence in support of any aspect of their case.

Party-appointed experts are required to be independent and to provide impartial evidence to assist the tribunal, rather than to support the party that appointed them as a 'hired gun'. Most arbitral rules contain certain minimum provisions regarding the use of experts, but it is advisable for the parties to supplement these by agreeing that the arbitral tribunal should be guided by more detailed rules such as the IBA Rules, which set out best practice for admission of evidence in international arbitration.[170] It is preferable for parties to appoint experts with whom either they or their counsel have prior experience, or at least for whom independent recommendations are available. This is especially so in the case of arbitrations concerning newer renewables technologies, where there have been relatively few large disputes and where experts may have little experience of testifying and undergoing cross-examination.

In addition to preparing a report for use in arbitration proceedings, experts can be effectively used behind the scenes as advisers to the parties in a number of areas:

- developing case strategy;
- conducting a preliminary assessment of a party's claim;
- helping to identify categories of relevant documents for production;
- drafting pleadings;

- assisting in preparation for the hearing, including questions for cross-examination of an opposing party's experts; and
- preparing closing submissions.

However, to the extent that any expert or team of analysts is assisting the main expert (ie, the expert who is on the record in the proceedings) with their report, caution should be exercised – the expert who is called for cross-examination needs to be able fully to explain their conclusions and the data underlying them, and so needs complete control over and awareness of any work done by others to assist in the preparation of their report.

The manner in which experts are deployed can also differ between civil and common law jurisdictions. This is something worth bearing in mind where the counterparty or the tribunal comes from a different legal background – they may have different practices and expectations that need to be taken into account.

It is particularly important in renewables arbitrations for parties to identify and engage technical experts early on, in order that any technical problems in the dispute, and how they will shape the proceedings, can be understood. Early engagement is also important given the relatively small field of available experts who have demonstrable and relevant experience of the new and emerging technologies used in the renewables sector. That small field is further limited by the need for experience in presenting oral evidence at a contested hearing, and such experts as have both availability and experience might in any event be constrained, by conflict of interest, from acting. It may therefore be necessary to engage experts who have a broader area of expertise, or who have experience with the same technology used in other applications, or outside the renewables context. For example, in the context of a dispute concerning defective welding at an onshore wind farm, it may be appropriate to engage an expert who has extensive knowledge of welding but no experience of onshore wind farms. In this respect, it is key to engage counsel who can recognise where parallels can be drawn with an expert's experience, and where there is a genuine gap in knowledge or experience that can affect an expert's credibility. This is critical, not only in respect of a party's own experts, but also in respect of experts appointed by a counterparty, in order that areas of vulnerability can be explored and exploited.

In every engagement with experts, it will be important that confidentiality and the requirements of legal privilege in communications are met. Great caution should be exercised in communications directly between parties and experts, which may well not meet the test for legal privilege and thus be vulnerable to having to be produced when it comes to the document production stage of an arbitration.

3.2 Tribunal-appointed experts

In certain circumstances, the arbitral tribunal might appoint its own expert to provide assistance on discrete issues. This is expressly allowed in many arbitration rules.[171] The role of a tribunal-appointed expert is flexible – but they might usefully prepare for the tribunal a summary of the issues in dispute where they are particularly complex.

The tribunal may also need access to an expert when writing its award. For example, where a renewables project employs a mathematical payment mechanism or particular software to calculate expected performance, the tribunal may need help translating their decision in law into such mechanism for their award to have practical meaning. Where this is a possibility, the parties should think about whether it is preferable for the party-appointed experts to assist the tribunal, or whether the tribunal should appoint its own expert. If the parties' experts are to assist, there should be ground rules in place as to how that process is to be managed to avoid either party having an additional opportunity – through its expert – to advance its case or get an insight into the tribunal's decision-making process, or even to get early notice as to what its decision will be.

In certain circumstances, the arbitral tribunal might appoint its own expert to provide assistance on discrete issues.

3.3 Ring-fencing relevant documents and witness evidence

Renewables projects have lifespans of many years or even decades. During that time, personnel with knowledge of the history of the dispute may leave the business, or relevant documents may be destroyed. Best practice record-keeping and paper trails are often key to evidencing a claim in a renewables dispute. Therefore, once a dispute becomes likely, it is important for parties to suspend any document destruction policies and to ring-fence any potentially relevant documents upon which they may need to rely, or which may be subject to production in due course. Similarly, taking statements from key witnesses early on is sensible – particularly where there is a risk they may leave the project.

With that in mind, parties must also be mindful of creating new documents or sharing any documents internally (such as with the board or any sponsors) that might be sensitive, given they might fall to be produced in document production in due course. Early engagement of counsel in this respect is key to protecting privilege as far as possible. In any event, it is important to think carefully before creating any new documents, and a good rule of thumb is not to create any new documents that you would not want your counterparty to see.

Allowing the tribunal to visit the site of a renewables project might also serve to emphasise the wider economic and political relevance of the project, or to give them a sense of scale or other potentially relevant information, like the accessibility of the site or the air quality.

3.4 Electronic and demonstrative exhibits

In technical disputes, electronic exhibits such as video presentations or drone footage can be particularly helpful tools for informing the tribunal. For example, renewables projects sometimes produce explanatory videos for visitors to the site or social media platforms which give an overview of the technology used at the project. Including these as electronic exhibits can help get the tribunal up to speed on the technical issues.

Similarly, demonstrative exhibits that incorporate visuals like photos, charts or videos can be helpful tools. Our experience is that these are particularly useful at the final merits hearing, when the legal team presents its oral opening submissions, or to accompany a presentation by an expert witness as part of their evidence-in-chief.

3.5 Site visits

In certain cases, site visits can be used to great effect, giving the tribunal a better understanding of the technical matters in dispute. For example, in a dispute concerning allegations of improper O&M, it might be helpful for the tribunal to visit the site and see first hand what operation of the plant involves. Allowing the tribunal to visit the site of a renewables project might also serve to emphasise the wider economic and political relevance of the project, or to give them a sense of scale or other potentially relevant information, like the accessibility of the site or the air quality.

If a site visit is to be conducted, it might be helpful to have any party- or tribunal-appointed experts on hand to answer any technical questions that the tribunal may have. Planning for the visit is also important – in order to avoid being caught by surprise, the parties should seek to agree in advance what the tribunal is to be shown, by whom, who will attend the visit on behalf of the parties, the extent to which legal counsel will be involved, what scope there will be for presentations and questions, and how and by whom any questions are to be answered.

4. Quantification of losses

The quantification of losses can be a lengthy and complicated process in the context of a renewables project, the aim often being to determine the fair market value of a project as at a particular valuation date.[172] There are a number of valuation methods that are employed to assess compensation, broadly separated into asset-based,[173] market-based[174] and income-based[175] approaches. There can be considerable uncertainty regarding this exercise, particularly in the case of renewables projects, where the need to take into account climate variables affecting projects creates complex models, and at least one and possibly multiple experts are likely to be required – both quantum and industry experts. For example, assessing the quantum of damages using the discounted cash flow method, widely used in energy arbitrations, requires a forecast of the anticipated future cash flows of a project, and identification of an appropriate discount rate. While oil and gas projects have a long history of reference to draw on in order to assess and estimate future losses, the same is not true for renewables projects, and the lack of comparable historical precedent makes the assessment of future damages a difficult and uncertain exercise. Further, most renewables projects are long term and so an appropriate discount rate might need to take into account the risk of regulatory changes, which can be hard to predict and which might require expert evidence on, for example, likely future tariffs based on the approach adopted in other comparable countries.

5. Identification of remedies and defects rectification

In particularly technical disputes involving malfunctioning equipment or processes, the remedy to be sought may not be entirely clear, especially at the outset of a dispute. In claims involving, for example, defective equipment, where the contract is silent or unclear, it may not be apparent whether the appropriate remedy is an order for the complete replacement of that equipment, or for specific repairs to be conducted. It may also not be clear whether the party responsible for the manufacture or installation of the equipment should implement the remedy, or whether an award of damages would be more appropriate to allow the injured party to implement a remedial solution itself. It is often helpful to seek expert assistance in determining the appropriate remedy, such as by providing an opinion on the works required to rectify a defect.

Parties should be mindful of the contractual regime governing defect rectification and in particular whether the contract requires them first to rectify any defects themselves before they can recover the cost of completed works from their counterparty; or whether they can request damages for the estimated cost of future works. Even if the latter approach is possible under the contract, it can produce evidential challenges in a disputes context.

At the same time, parties should take care that any steps they do take do not prejudice their position in the arbitration in due course. For example, failing to take action to rectify defects might be characterised as a failure to mitigate loss, while taking mitigating steps might undermine a claim that replacement of the defective works is what is required. Replacing and repairing equipment is also fraught with risk that the opposition will argue that the damages sought represent an impermissible claim for betterment, rather than a claim for compensation for loss actually suffered as a result of the breach. Following the advice of appropriately qualified experts is critical in this respect.

While oil and gas projects have a long history of reference to draw on in order to assess and estimate future losses, the same is not true for renewables projects, and the lack of comparable historical precedent makes the assessment of future damages a difficult and uncertain exercise.

6. Third-party funding

Renewables cases often result in large damages awards, but can be costly to fund. Parties looking to commence an arbitration might find assistance through a third-party funder, who will contribute to the costs of the arbitration in return for a share of any damages awarded. Parties should, however, be mindful of how such arrangements are treated across different jurisdictions. In the United Kingdom, for example, the Supreme Court's ruling in *PACCAR* has restricted funders from charging success fees calculated as a percentage of damages awarded,[176] although there has been discussion about reversing the effect of this finding through legislation.

7. ADR techniques

The long lifespan of a renewables project makes maintaining a cordial relationship with contracting parties an important consideration in the event of a dispute. It may not be an option for one party simply to exit the project, and parties may need to continue working together for decades after a dispute arises. The incorporation of other ADR methods at key stages of the arbitration process can be helpful in exploring the possibility of an early settlement in order to save costs, giving the parties greater level of control over the outcome and providing them with an opportunity to rebuild and move forward in their relationship. Ultimately, the effectiveness of any ADR process depends on the parties' willingness meaningfully to engage with the process. Common ADR techniques are outlined below.

7.1 Mediation

Mediation at an appropriate stage in the arbitration might be helpful in resolving discrete issues, or even disposing of the dispute entirely. Mediation is a relatively inexpensive process and can save significant time and cost if it results in an early negotiated settlement. The parties might usefully participate in one or more mediations, covering either the entire range of issues or specific problems. Mediations are generally private and without prejudice, such that parties can discuss freely the issues in dispute and make concessions without compromising their position in the broader arbitration. However, the extent of any without prejudice protection may differ between jurisdictions, and parties should take care when preparing for a mediation that they do not create documents that might be required to be produced in the arbitration in due course. Generally, it is best to be clear at the outset and record in writing how the discussions and any documents produced for the mediation are to be treated. Mediators are not usually expected to formally express an opinion on the merits, but might nevertheless share privately with the parties their views on the issues in dispute.

There is a delicate balance involved as to when is the best time for a mediation to take place. A particularly complex and technical dispute may need evidence to be exchanged, or document production to occur, prior to the mediation in order to be meaningful. If mediation is proposed too soon and the parties have not yet had the opportunity fully to digest their opponent's case, the parties may not understand what they need from the mediation process in order to resolve the dispute. If proposed too late, the parties may become entrenched in their positions, or the evidence may strongly favour one party, which makes negotiation and compromise difficult; or the parties may have already incurred a level of cost that renders the cost-saving aspect of a mediation redundant.

If the mediation results in a binding settlement agreement, the parties might agree to have the agreement included in a consent award or partial award, allowing it to be enforced as an arbitral award, rather than relying on the enforcement of a contractual settlement. This is expressly anticipated in the rules of many arbitral institutions.[177]

Even if not ultimately successful, mediation can be useful in encouraging the parties to consider what they really need from the dispute resolution process, and may narrow the issues in dispute.

7.2 Facilitation, conciliation and expert determination of key issues

In more complicated cases, parties might consider a facilitation, which identifies the key steps needed to resolve a dispute; or a conciliation, which allows a third party to express his or her non-binding views on the dispute and potential settlement options.[178] Expert determination of key issues might also be usefully deployed in a dispute involving discrete technical issues that can be dealt with individually, for example, in a case involving hundreds of delay or variation claims, expert determination might resolve a proportion of the claims in the interests of efficiency.

8. Virtual hearings

A major change to arbitration following the COVID-19 pandemic has been the increased prevalence of virtual and hybrid arbitration hearings. This is a welcome development: hybrid hearings reduce the need for participants to travel to attend hearings (in line with the Campaign for Greener Arbitrations)[179] and mean that witnesses and key personnel can remain on site when giving evidence – a particularly important consideration in renewables arbitrations where witnesses are often engineers or managers who need to remain on site to keep the project running.

Even if not ultimately successful, mediation can be useful in encouraging the parties to consider what they really need from the dispute resolution process, and may narrow the issues in dispute.

There are challenges, however, with conducting remote or hybrid hearings, largely related to failures in communications technology. Any technical problems can distract the tribunal from the message being conveyed by the witness at the time. A trial run is the best way to guard against this risk – any witnesses or experts testifying remotely should participate in at least one dry run to make sure the technology works and they are familiar with the information they will see on screen. It is important to pay attention to 'scene dressing'; things like the lights turning off automatically, fire alarm tests, a prominent painting behind a witness and whether the witness or expert is looking directly at the camera or constantly looking down at notes may seem like minor points, but can be a source of distraction nevertheless.

If a virtual or hybrid hearing is likely, then agreeing a virtual hearing protocol beforehand is important. Such protocols typically cover issues like the minimum standard of equipment and technology to be used by remote participants; how any translators will be involved; and practical measures for how witnesses will give evidence virtually (eg, whether they will be permitted to have hard copies of any documents in front of them, and whether other individuals may be present in the room to provide technical assistance).

VII. Looking over the horizon: the future of renewables arbitrations

The renewable energy sector is dynamic and evolving. As the energy transition progresses, the introduction of new technology, new players and new regulations means the sector will need to adapt in order to address new risks and challenges. For the reasons explored in this report, international arbitration is well suited to resolving the many and varied disputes that will continue to arise as the transition progresses.

1. Energy transition: more claims

The shift towards a greater proportion of renewable energy in the global mix will inevitably result in more disputes of the type discussed throughout this report. This sentiment is echoed by the findings of Ashurst LLP's Powering Change Report 2024, where a significant majority – more than two-thirds of those surveyed – confirmed that they expect to see an increase in legal disputes over the coming years.[180]

1.1 Technology disputes

The number of disputes concerning technical problems arising on renewables projects will undoubtedly increase as new and experimental technologies develop and are quickly upscaled for deployment at a commercial scale.

As the energy transition progresses, the introduction of new technology, new players and new regulations means the sector will need to adapt in order to address new risks and challenges.

Wind power has a particularly crucial role to play in decarbonising energy markets, and a significant increase in installed wind power capacity globally is anticipated. The United Kingdom is at the forefront of wind power development and has committed to almost doubling its wind capacity, including, significantly, through offshore turbines and the pioneering use of floating installations. Despite progress in its development, floating offshore wind technology is still in its nascent stages. Currently, there are no turbines specifically designed for floating applications. Instead, fixed-bottom turbines are being adapted for use in floating wind farm demos and proposals. Moreover, the installed capacity of projects concluded to date (and the size of turbines used in those projects) has been relatively modest compared to the more ambitious proposals for future installations. The use of existing technologies in such new and significantly scaled-up applications is likely to be a key driver of commercial disputes, as has been the case with the scaling-up of solar PV and the deployment of CSP, where commercial disputes have arisen as a result of the relatively untried and untested nature of the technology and/or its application.

Green hydrogen (that is, hydrogen produced through renewable energy sources) is also projected to play a pivotal role in the transition towards a low-carbon economy, given its potential to decarbonise industries that currently depend heavily on fossil fuels, like transport. Low-emission hydrogen production is already expanding rapidly: the number of announced low-emission projects is growing,[181] as is the development of electrolysers used for hydrogen production.[182] Despite the robust interest in green hydrogen technology, it is important to recognise that it is still in its relative infancy. The nascent stage of development carries inherent uncertainties, which could give rise to disputes resulting from unforeseen challenges in the technology. There may also be regulatory and quality-related disputes in the future over whether hydrogen is truly 'green'.

Climate change mitigation strategies are also projected to depend heavily on carbon dioxide removal (CDR) strategies,[183] which are also in the early stages of development. The risks associated with upscaling such existing technologies are not fully understood, again leading to potential disputes risk.

Intellectual property disputes will likely be more prevalent as novel technologies are invented and developed. The speed and scale of innovation required means companies will likely need to collaborate to develop ideas. There is ample scope for disputes arising out of such relationships, including over intellectual property ownership and the sharing of any royalties. Working with counsel to ensure that intellectual property rights are proactively protected is critical.

1.2 Regulatory change

Energy policy is in a state of flux as governments across the globe pursue green agendas. Governments' increased focus on renewables may mean greater pressure on companies to roll out projects quickly, increasing the disputes risk. For example, the new Labour government in the United Kingdom has declared an intention of becoming a "clean energy superpower" and achieving zero-carbon electricity by 2030. This is a challenging target, and will require significant upgrading of the electricity grid and associated infrastructure. The government intends to partner with the private sector to achieve this objective and has established Great British Energy, a publicly owned clean power company, to join with private companies in developing renewable energy projects. The tight timeframes and increased political oversight from this endeavour will no doubt put pressure on the private sector and may result in claims when new projects encounter problems down the line.

To date, government subsidies have supported the growth of new renewables technologies and markets, and it is anticipated that many governments will continue to introduce or maintain support regimes to encourage foreign direct investment in renewables as part of climate change mitigation efforts.

There is, however, a risk that some existing support mechanisms will be changed or removed entirely, or that new taxes and levies will be imposed on renewable energy generation, which might have adverse implications for entrenched players. For example, a number of countries, including the United States and Australia, have offered incentive schemes and subsidies for carbon capture, use and storage technologies. As seen in Europe, where subsidies are offered to incentivise investment in the solar sector in particular, these schemes can become victims of their own success. Once they have attracted sufficient investment, governments may find that they need to be scaled back, or withdrawn altogether, as their widespread use can result in cost to the state that can no longer be justified. This, in turn, could lead to investment treaty disputes.

Ultimately, there is a real risk of governments making legal and regulatory changes to reduce the level of support offered to players in the renewables sector, which may lead to disputes where investor-state conduct is expropriatory, or done without regard to the legitimate expectations of existing investors. As climate change, and the need for states to take action to meet their commitments, becomes an accepted risk factor in the industry, this may impact investors' legitimate expectations and consequently their ability to successfully claim damages for breach of IIAs. Indeed, it is likely that there will be an increased focus in investor-state jurisprudence on the tension between a state's right to regulate for the purpose of furthering climate change mitigation efforts, and investors' legitimate expectation of a stable regulatory framework. There may also be a focus on how the right to regulate should take account of changed economic circumstances, and potentially a revisiting of 'doctrine of necessity' arguments to defend against claims, on the basis that climate change justifies dramatic changes in the scale of support offered for energy projects.

1.3 Decommissioning disputes

A necessary corollary of the increase in renewable energy projects is the phasing down and out of fossil-fuelled projects. The science in this respect is clear – "all fossil fuels must be effectively phased out to secure a safe and liveable future".[184] In practical terms, this means that many fossil fuel projects currently planned or under development are at risk of being stranded as the transition progresses.[185] Investors will no doubt look to their rights under IIAs where decommissioning activities are prompted by legal or regulatory change precluding oil and gas activity, preventing the further grant of concessions and licences (or indeed cancelling existing permissions), taxing those activities or withdrawing whatever financial support mechanisms might still underpin them.

The decommissioning of oil and gas assets is a complicated and expensive exercise, and decommissioning may well face environmental and societal, as well as technical, regulatory and economic challenges. Disputes might arise in relation to hand-back obligations in concession agreements, payment on termination, or ownership of equipment at the end of a project. There is ample scope for disputes, both at investor-state level (as impacted investors pursue claims under relevant IIAs) and commercial level (noting that some standard form decommissioning contracts have been developed that provide for the arbitration of disputes).[186]

Under public international law, claims will likely be based on the fair and equitable treatment standard, unreasonable or discriminatory measures, and indirect expropriation. This is already an area where states have seen substantial claims under the ECT – the *Rockhopper v Italy* tribunal, as mentioned above, awarded nearly €200 million (including nearly €7 million in decommissioning costs) to an investor in Italy after it had been denied a production concession to exploit an offshore oil field, finding that Italy had committed an unlawful expropriation.[187]

Similar issues might arise in relation to the upgrading of existing renewable energy projects. In the onshore wind industry, for example, many projects are reaching the end of their operational life cycle.

Given the demand for increased capacity globally, the equipment in these projects may need to be upgraded or replaced to meet states' net zero targets. These 'repowering' projects will not be straightforward and disputes could result from the need to reapply for licences and consents, as well as from the physical upgrade works themselves (particularly in circumstances where technology has moved on significantly from when those projects were first conceived).

2. Geopolitical factors

The renewables sector is particularly vulnerable to geopolitical events, and the supply chain disruption and wider market changes they can cause. The sector has seen significant disruption in recent years from the COVID-19 pandemic (the impact of which is still being felt in the construction sector), the Russia–Ukraine war and related imposition of sanctions, and disruption to global shipping routes. These tumultuous events have impacted global supply chains and caused record-high energy prices, inflation and interest rates. They have prompted states to re-evaluate their energy portfolios, prioritising self-reliance and energy security. To this end, states have made a concerted effort to diversify energy sources, moving away from reliance on Russian natural gas, adopting alternatives such as liquefied

The renewables sector is particularly vulnerable to geopolitical events, and the supply chain disruption and wider market changes they can cause.

natural gas, and accelerating their expansion of new renewable energy capacity.[188] In some cases states have diverted efforts away from renewables and refocused on, for example, nuclear energy. In the short to medium term, the ripple effects of the Russia–Ukraine war are most likely to be seen in legal claims arising out of suspended contractual performance, as well as price review claims. Disputes may also relate to claims for prolongation and disruption costs or extensions of time based on changes in contract law or *force majeure* provisions.

Relatedly, the energy transition will likely see an increase in commodities disputes, particularly in the mining sector. The energy transition will require billions of tonnes of critical minerals and metals for the manufacture of clean energy technologies, including solar panels, wind turbines and batteries.[189] Demand for minerals is expected to quadruple by 2040.[190] These critical minerals are concentrated in a handful of countries, most of which are developing nations, with global supply largely controlled by Chinese companies. Renewables projects are therefore particularly vulnerable to supply chain disruption, which can in turn cause a raft of downstream disputes, including claims for additional time and cost and relief from contractual performance obligations. The rare minerals sector is also anticipated to be subject to heightened state control (the Mexican government, for example, recently cancelled nine lithium concessions previously held by a Chinese company in order to exert greater control over lithium resources),[191] potentially leading to more investor–state claims.

3. Intra-European investor–state arbitration

As discussed in Chapter I, investor–state arbitration in Europe is becoming increasingly challenging. In the short to medium term, the ECT is likely to remain the key IIA for investors in the renewable energy industry affected by regulatory changes, who are seeking relief against host states. For now, arbitration tribunals are generally continuing to uphold their own jurisdiction to determine intra-EU arbitrations, but successful investors are facing difficulties at the enforcement stage. However, investors should closely monitor developments in this space, and in the meantime should consider whether they have – or can restructure to gain – protection under an alternative IIA with a non-European signatory. Future arbitrations may consider, in particular, the validity of current attempts to disapply the ECT's sunset provision.

Similarly, while the ECT modernisation discussions have stalled, with many states choosing to withdraw rather than agree the proposed amendments, other existing IIAs might be modified to give greater latitude to governments to regulate in accordance with climate change mitigation and adaptation efforts in order to address concerns regarding the alleged chilling effect of investor–state arbitration. Amendments to other BITs and MITs might frame the protection of states' right to regulate in more robust terms, or include provisions carving out domestic climate change measures from the scope of protection.

4. Changes to arbitration

The ongoing evolution of the renewable energy sector offers many lessons for the international arbitration community. As the sector matures, we might see the development of specialised rules and guidance tailored to renewable energy disputes. This would reflect the call made by the IBA in its Climate Change Justice and Human Rights Report for action to be taken to ensure that arbitration procedures are fit for the purpose of addressing the complexities of climate change disputes.[192]

Further, the need for renewables disputes to be resolved promptly and meaningfully may promote a shift in procedural practices amongst the arbitration community. Mediation and other ADR methods may play a larger role; the use of technical experts as arbitrators may increase as understanding the technical aspects of disputes becomes more important; and there may be a stronger push towards the publication of arbitration awards (on an anonymised basis) to promote transparency with respect to decisions concerning energy transition-related issues. There is also likely to be a greater focus on the use of artificial intelligence in arbitration, including in arbitrator selection, case analysis and the management of document production.

International arbitration is set to remain the leading dispute resolution mechanism for renewables disputes in the long term. It remains an efficient, accessible and flexible process that can assist the global transition to a low-carbon economy.

Notes

1 UN Environment Programme (UNEP), "Emissions Gap Report 2023" (2023), Executive Summary, pxix, www.unep.org/resources/emissions-gap-report-2023.
2 The 'emissions gap' measures the difference between the level of greenhouse gas emissions that the world needs to achieve to avoid the worst impacts of climate change and the projected levels of greenhouse emissions based on current national commitments to decarbonisation: UNEP, "Emissions Gap Report 2023", *supra*, Foreword, pxv.
3 UNEP, "Annual Report 2023" (2023), p7, www.unep.org/resources/annual-report-2023.
4 UNEP, "Emissions Gap Report 2023", *supra*, ppxvi, xxii and xxiii.
5 *Ibid*, pxxv.
6 *Ibid*, pxvii.
7 International Energy Agency (IEA), "Net Zero Roadmap" (2023), Executive Summary, p16, www.iea.org/reports/net-zero-roadmap-a-global-pathway-to-keep-the-15-0c-goal-in-reach.
8 IEA, "COP28: Tracking the Energy Outcomes", www.iea.org/topics/cop28-tracking-the-energy-outcomes.
9 United Nations Framework Convention on Climate Change (UNFCCC), "Report of the Conference of the Parties serving as the meeting of the Parties to the Paris Agreement on its fifth session, held in the United Arab Emirates from 30 November to 13 December 2023", paragraph 28 (a), unfccc.int/documents/637073.
10 International Renewable Energy Agency (IRENA), "Renewable Capacity Statistics 2024" (2024), Foreword, www.irena.org/Publications/2024/Mar/Renewable-capacity-statistics-2024.
11 IEA, "COP28: Tracking the Energy Outcomes", *supra*.
12 Ashurst LLP, "Powering Change: Technologies fuelling the future" (2024), Chapter 1, p7, www.ashurst.com/en/powering-change-technologies-fuelling-the-future/.
13 *Ibid*, Chapter 1, p12.
14 IEA, "World Energy Investment 2024" (2024), p59, www.iea.org/reports/world-energy-investment-2024.
15 IEA, "Renewable 2023" (2023), p7, www.iea.org/reports/renewables-2023.
16 As opposed to energy generated using coal, oil or gas.
17 Other technologies that are not discussed include hydropower, geothermal, ocean energy, biogas and green hydrogen:

- Hydropower is energy derived from flowing water. Hydroelectric power plants generate electricity by passing flowing water through a turbine. Rivers are used in small-scale hydro projects, but larger hydroelectric power projects use dams and reservoirs to store water as potential energy. Hydropower technology is relatively mature (with a history dating back 2,000 years), and is today one of the most cost-effective means of generating electricity. Hydropower currently represents the largest share of global renewable generation capacity.
- Geothermal energy is heat from the earth's subsurface. Geothermal energy is carried to the surface in water or steam, for example by pumping hot water from underground aquifers into pipes. This energy can be used directly for heating or to generate electricity using steam. The main advantage of geothermal energy is that it is not dependent on weather conditions (unlike wind and solar technologies).
- Ocean-based technologies use converters to capture energy contained in ocean waves to generate electricity. Tidal energy is produced by technologies that capture energy from water moving between two different heights with the daily tide using a barrage; other ocean technologies use the temperature difference between warmer surface seawater and colder subsurface seawater, or the salinity gradient where freshwater streams meet saline seawater, to generate electricity.
- Biogas is gas produced from biomass using advanced conversion technologies (ACTs) such as gasification, pyrolysis or anaerobic digestion, which break down organic material into methane, carbon dioxide and other residues. The methane can be combusted to generate electricity.
- Hydrogen is an 'energy carrier', which means that it can store energy for conversion into other forms of energy at a later stage. 'Green' hydrogen is produced using renewable electricity to split water into hydrogen and oxygen in an electrolyser (electrolysis), or through the gasification of biomass.

18 New and emerging technologies include, for example: ocean energy technologies, floating solar power plants, floating wind farms, air storage technologies, bladeless wind turbines and airborne wind energy systems.
19 Ashurst LLP, "Powering Change: Technologies fuelling the future", *supra*, Chapter 1, p11. For example, in 2022 the United Kingdom government committed to installing 5GW of floating offshore wind capacity by 2030, which is a significant commitment given the relatively modest capacity installed to date.
20 Michelle Froese, "Risky Business: Mitigating threats to onshore wind projects & portfolios", *Wind Power Engineering and Development*, 20 February 2018, www.windpowerengineering.com/risky-business-mitigating-threats-onshore-wind-projects-portfolios.
21 Paul Gerke, "Offshore wind cancellations put goal of 30 GW by 2030 out of reach", *Renewable Energy World*, 9 July 2024, www.renewableenergyworld.com/wind-power/offshore-wind-cancellations-put-goal-of-30-gw-by-2030-out-of-reach/#gref.
22 Michael Race, BBC News, "No bids for offshore wind in government auction", 8 September 2023, www.bbc.co.uk/news/business-66749344.

23 There is no wind turbine designed specifically for use in a floating installation – instead, fixed-bottom turbines are being used in floating offshore project proposals, the scale of which has to date been in the tens of megawatts and nowhere near the tens of gigawatts that are envisaged over the next five years.
24 PPP Risk Allocation, "Photovoltaic Solar Plant", https://ppp-risk.gihub.org/risk-allocation-matrix/energy/photovoltaic-solar-plant/.
25 Parabolic trough technology uses a solar 'field' of curved (parabolic) mirrors (or 'troughs') that concentrate sunlight onto a central receiver tube containing a synthetic heat transfer fluid, which is used to heat water and generate superheated steam. The mirrors can be static or move to track the sun.
26 Enclosed trough systems enclose parabolic mirrors within 'glasshouse' structures, which protect the mirrors from wind and dust that negatively affects the mirrors' reflectivity (and therefore their efficiency). The technology generally produces steam directly (rather than using a heat transfer fluid) by concentrating sunlight onto pipes containing water.
27 Linear Fresnel reflector (LFR) technology uses flat or slightly curved mirror strips to concentrate sunlight onto absorbers using the Fresnel lens effect, and generally produces steam directly.
28 Solar power tower technology uses a field of mirrored heliostats to concentrate sunlight onto a central receiver positioned on top of a tower, containing a heat transfer fluid or molten salt which is used to superheat steam.
29 Dish engine or dish Stirling technology uses a single parabolic dish reflector to concentrate light onto a receiver positioned at the focal point. The receiver captures heat, which is converted to electricity using a Stirling engine.
30 The Green Climate Fund (GCF) was established by the UNFCCC to support adaptation and mitigation efforts by financing low-emissions projects in developing countries: Green Climate Fund, "About GCF" (2020), www.greenclimate.fund/about.
31 UNEP, "Adaptation Gap Report 2023" (2023), pxi, www.unep.org/resources/adaptation-gap-report-2023.
32 United Nations Conference on Trade and Development (UNCTAD), International Investment Agreements Navigator, https://investmentpolicy.unctad.org/international-investment-agreements.
33 The ECT is available at www.energycharter.org/fileadmin/DocumentsMedia/Legal/ECTC-en.pdf.
34 The Energy Charter Treaty (ECT), adopted in Lisbon in December 1994, regulates "economic activity' in the energy sector", which is defined in Article 1(5) as "an economic activity concerning the exploration, extraction, refining, production, storage, land transport, transmission, distribution, trade, marketing, or sale of Energy Materials and Products except those included in Annex NI, or concerning the distribution of heat to multiple premises". Article 1(4) of the ECT states that "Energy Materials and Products" are the items included in Annexes EM I and EM II, which include "electrical energy" at item 27.16.
35 *Ibid*, Preamble.
36 Afghanistan, Albania, Armenia, Austria, Azerbaijan, Belarus, Belgium, Bosnia and Herzegovina, Bulgaria, Croatia, Cyprus, Czech Republic, Denmark, Estonia, European Union and Euratom, Finland, Georgia, Greece, Hungary, Iceland, Ireland, Japan, Jordan, Kazakhstan, Kyrgyzstan, Latvia, Liechtenstein, Lithuania, Luxembourg, Malta, Moldova, Mongolia, Montenegro, the Netherlands, North Macedonia, Norway, Portugal, Romania, Slovakia, Slovenia, Spain, Sweden, Switzerland, Tajikistan, Turkey, Turkmenistan, Ukraine, United Kingdom, Uzbekistan and Yemen. Australia has signed the treaty but notified of its intention not to become a party. Russia signed the ECT but did not ratify it and, in 2009, confirmed that it did not intend to become a contracting party and terminated its provisional application with effect from 18 October 2009. Italy, France, Germany and Poland have notified their withdrawal from the treaty, but the provisions of the ECT regarding dispute settlement remain in force for 20 years pursuant to Article 47(3) of the ECT.
37 'Investor' is defined in Article 1(7) of the ECT as either "a natural person having the citizenship or nationality of or who is permanently residing in" a state that is a contracting party to the ECT "in accordance with its applicable law", or "a company or other organisation organised in accordance with the law applicable" in that state. Article 1(6) of the ECT defines 'investment' as "every kind of asset, owned or controlled directly or indirectly by an investor" and lists examples including:

- tangible and intangible, moveable and immoveable property, and any property rights such as leases, mortgages, liens and pledges;
- a company or business enterprise, or shares, stock or other forms of equity participation in a company or business enterprise, and bonds and other debt of a company or business enterprise;
- claims to money and claims to performance pursuant to a contract having an economic value and associated with an 'investment';
- 'intellectual property' (which is defined in Article 1(12) of the ECT as including "copyrights and related rights, trademarks, geographical indications, industrial designs, patents, layout designs of integrated circuits and the protection of undisclosed information");
- 'returns' (which is defined in Article 1(12) of the ECT as including "copyrights and related rights, trademarks, geographical indications, industrial designs, patents, layout designs of integrated circuits and the protection of undisclosed information"); and
- any right conferred by law or contract or by virtue of any licences and permits granted pursuant to law to undertake any "economic activity in the energy sector".

38 'Expropriation' is in essence the taking of private property by a government acting in its sovereign capacity, or matters having equivalent effect: Mark W Friedman, Dietmar W Prager and Ina C Popova, "Expropriation and Nationalisation", in J William Rowley *et al* (eds), *The Guide to Energy Arbitrations* (*Global Arbitration Review*, 2015), p18.

39 ECT, Article 13(1)(a).
40 ECT, Article 13(1)(c).
41 'Direct' expropriation involves the actual taking of an investment, and usually involves a deliberate intent – eg, a state directly transferring legal title in an asset to itself. A classic case of direct expropriation was the subject of the award in *Kardassopoulos v Georgia*. In that case, Georgia terminated a 30-year concession agreement in respect of its main oil pipeline and transferred the rights in the project to a state-owned entity without due process of law and without compensation. This was found to be an unlawful direct expropriation of the claimant's investment, in violation of the ECT: *Kardassopoulos v Georgia* (ICSID Case Nos ARB/05/18 and ARB/07/15) (Award dated 3 March 2010), para 387.
42 'Indirect' expropriation claims are more common. Indirect expropriation involves a measure or series of measures by a state which taken together amount to expropriation. Some IIAs expressly offer protection against indirect expropriation. See, eg, Article 4(1) of the Agreement between the Republic of Austria and the Great Socialist People's Libyan Arab Jamahiriya for the Promotion and Protection of Investments (Vienna, 18 June 2002): "A Contracting Party shall not expropriate or nationalise *directly or indirectly* an investment of an investor of the other Contracting Party or take any measures having equivalent effect" (emphasis added).
43 *Rockhopper Exploration Plc, Rockhopper Italia SPA and Rockhopper Mediterranean Ltd v Italian Republic* (ICSID Case No ARB/17/14) (Final Award dated 23 August 2022).
44 See, eg, *ESPF Beteiligungs GmbH, ESPF Nr. 2 Austria Beteiligungs GmbH, and InfraClass Energie 5 GmbH & Co KG v Italian Republic* (ICSID Case No ARB/16/5) (Award dated 14 September 2020), para 443; *Electrabel SA v Hungary* (ICSID Case No ARB/07/19) (Award dated 25 November 2015), para 7.74; *Walter Bau AG (In Liquidation) v Kingdom of Thailand* (UNCITRAL Award dated 1 July 2009), para 11.5; and *Ioan Micula, Viorel Micula, SC European Food SA, SC Starmill SRL and SC Multipack SRL v Romania* (ICSID Case No ARB/05/20) (Award dated 11 December 2013), paras 502–521.
45 Nigel Blackaby *et al*, *Redfern and Hunter on International Arbitration*, 6th edition (Oxford University Press, 2015), para 8.96.
46 ECT, Article 10(1).
47 *ESPF Beteiligungs Gmbh, ESPF Nr 2 Austraia Beteiligungs Gmbh and Infraclass Energie 5 GMBh & Co KG v Italian Republic* (ICSID Case No ARB/16/5) (Award dated 14 September 2020).
48 *El Paso Energy International Co v Argentine Republic* (ICSID Case No ARB/03/15) (Award dated 31 October 2011), paras 522–523. This passage was applied in *Electrabel SA v Republic of Hungary* (ICSID Case No ARB/07/19) (Award dated 25 November 2015) at para 7.83.
49 *Strabag SE v Libya* (ICSID Case No ARB(AF)/15/1) (Award dated 29 June 2020).
50 *Global Arbitration Review*, "More Egyptian claims in the pipeline" (8 May 2012), https://globalarbitrationreview.com/article/1031321/more-egyptian-claims-in-the-pipeline.
51 See, eg, ECT, Article 10(1).
52 *ESPF Beteiligungs GmbH, ESPF Nr. 2 Austria Beteiligungs GmbH and InfraClass Energie 5 GmbH & Co KG v Italian Republic* (ICSID Case No ARB/16/5) (Award dated 14 September 2020), paras 811 and 821.
53 See ECT, Article 26.
54 The Convention on the Settlement of Investment Disputes between States and Nationals of Other States (Washington, 1966).
55 *CSP Equity Investment Sarl v Kingdom of Spain* (SCC Case No 094/2013); *Isolux Infrastructure Netherlands BV v Kingdom of Spain* (SCC Case No 2013/153); *The PV Investors v Kingdom of Spain* (PCA Case No 2012-14); *Charanne BV and Construction Investments Sarl v Kingdom of Spain* (SCC Case No 062/2012); *RREEF Infrastructure (GP) Ltd and RREEF Pan-European Infrastructure Two Lux Sarl v Kingdom of Spain* (ICSID Case No ARB/13/30); *Antin Infrastructure Services Luxembourg Sarl and Antin Energia Termosolar BV v Kingdom of Spain* (ICSID Case No ARB/13/31); *Eiser Infrastructure Ltd and Energía Solar Luxembourg Sarl v Kingdom of Spain* (ICSID Case No ARB/13/36); *Masdar Solar & Wind Cooperatief UA v Kingdom of Spain* (ICSID Case No ARB/14/1); *NextEra Energy Global Holdings BV and NextEra Energy Spain Holdings BV v Kingdom of Spain* (ICSID Case No ARB/14/11); *InfraRed Environmental Infrastructure GP Ltd v Kingdom of Spain* (ICSID Case No ARB/14/12); *Novenergia II – Energy & Environment (SCA), SICAR v Kingdom of Spain* (SCC Case No 063/2015); *Foresight Luxembourg Solar 1 Sarl, Foresight Luxembourg Solar 2 Sarl, Greentech Energy System A/S, GWM Renewable Energy I SPA and GWM Renewable Energy II SPA v Kingdom of Spain* (SCC Case No 2015/150); *Landesbank Baden-Württemberg, HSH Nordbank AG, Landesbank Hessen-Thüringen Girozentrale and Norddeutsche Landesbank-Girozentrale v Kingdom of Spain* (ICSID Case No ARB/15/45); *Watkins Holdings Sarl v Kingdom of Spain* (ICSID Case No ARB/15/44); *Hydro Energy 1 Sarl and Hydroxana Sweden AB v Kingdom of Spain* (ICSID Case No ARB/15/42); *SolEs Badajoz GmbH v Kingdom of Spain* (ICSID Case No ARB/15/38); *RENERGY Sarl v Kingdom of Spain* (ICSID Case No ARB/14/18); *RWE Innogy GmbH and RWE Innogy Aersa SAU v Kingdom of Spain* (ICSID Case No ARB/14/34); *Stadtwerke München GmbH v Kingdom of Spain* (ICSID Case No ARB/15/1); *STEAG GmbH v Kingdom of Spain* (ICSID Case No ARB/15/4); *Alten Renewable Energy Developments BV v Kingdom of Spain* (SCC Case No 2015/036); *9REN Holding Sarl v Kingdom of Spain* (ICSID Case No ARB/15/15); *BayWa r.e. Renewable Energy GmbH and BayWa r.e. Asset Holding GmbH v Kingdom of Spain* (ICSID Case No ARB/15/16); *Cube Infrastructure Fund SICAV v Kingdom of Spain* (ICSID Case No ARB/15/20); *Matthias Kruck v Kingdom of Spain* (ICSID Case No ARB/15/23); *KS Invest GmbH and TLS Invest GmbH v Kingdom of Spain* (ICSID Case No ARB/15/25); *Solarpark Management GmbH & Co Atum I KG v Kingdom of Spain* (SCC Case No

2015/163); *Eurus Energy Holdings Corp and Eurus Energy Europe BV v Kingdom of Spain* (ICSID Case No ARB/16/4); *Aharon Naftali Biram, Gilatz Spain SL, Redmill Holdings Ltd and Sun-Flower Olmeda GmbH v Kingdom of Spain* (ICSID Case No ARB/16/17); *Infracapital F1 Sarl and Infracapital Solar BV v Kingdom of Spain* (ICSID Case No ARB/16/18); *Cordoba Beheer BV, Cross Retail SL, Sevilla Beheer BV, Spanish Project Companies v Kingdom of Spain* (ICSID Case No ARB/16/27); *Green Power K/S and Obton A/S v Kingdom of Spain* (SCC Case No 2016/135); *European Solar Farms A/S v Kingdom of Spain* (ICSID Case No ARB/18/45); *Canepa Green Energy Opportunities I, Sarl and Canepa Green Energy Opportunities II, Sarl v Kingdom of Spain* (ICSID Case No ARB/19/4); *Sapec, SA v Kingdom of Spain* (ICSID Case No ARB/19/23); *M Solar GmbH & Co KG, M Solar Verwaltungs GmbH, Solarizz Holding GmbH & Co KG v Kingdom of Spain* (ICSID Case No ARB/19/30); *OperaFund Eco-Invest SICAV plc and Schwab Holding AG v Kingdom of Spain* (ICSID Case No ARB/15/36); *E.ON SE, E.ON Finanzanlagen GmbH and E.ON Iberia Holding GmbH v Kingdom of Spain* (ICSID Case No ARB/15/35); *Cavalum SGPS, SA v Kingdom of Spain* (ICSID Case No ARB/15/34); *JGC Corp v Kingdom of Spain* (ICSID Case No ARB/15/27); *Itochu Corp v Kingdom of Spain* (ICSID Case No ARB/18/25); *EBL (Genossenschaft Elektra Baselland) and Tubo Sol PE2 SL v Spain*; (ICSID Case No ARB/18/42); *EDF Energies Nouvelles SA v Spain* (PCA Case No AA613); *Triodos SICAV II v Kingdom of Spain* (SCC Case No 2017-194); *Portigon AG v Kingdom of Spain* (ICSID Case No ARB/17/15); *DCM Energy GmbH & Co Solar 1 KG, DCM Energy GmbH & Co Solar 2 KG, Edisun Power Europe AG, Hannover Leasing Sun Invest 2 Spanien Beteiligungs GmbH, and Hannover Leasing Sun Invest 2 Spanien GmbH & Co KG v Kingdom of Spain* (ICSID Case No ARB/17/41); *FREIF Eurowind v Spain* (SCC Case No 2017/060); *Mitsui & Co Ltd v Kingdom of Spain* (ICSID Case No ARB/20/47); *WOC Photovoltaik Portfolio GmbH & Co. KG and others v Kingdom of Spain* (ICSID Case No ARB/22/12); *Spanish Solar 1 Limited and Spanish Solar 2 Limited v Kingdom of Spain* (ICSID Case No ARB/21/39); and *TS Villalba GmbH and others v Kingdom of Spain* (ICSID Case No ARB/21/43).

56 *CSP Equity Investment Sarl v Kingdom of Spain* (SCC Case No 094/2013); *Isolux Infrastructure Netherlands BV v Kingdom of Spain* (SCC Case No 2013/153) (Award dated 12 July 2016); *Charanne BV and Construction Investments Sarl v Kingdom of Spain* (SCC Case No 062/2012) (Award dated 21 January 2016); *Stadtwerke München GmbH v Kingdom of Spain* (ICSID Case No ARB/15/1) (Award dated 2 December 2019); *Green Power K/S and Obton A/S v Kingdom of Spain* (SCC Case No 2016/135); and *FREIF Eurowind Holdings Ltd v Kingdom of Spain* (SCC Case No 2017/060) (Final Award dated 8 March 2021).

57 *Eiser Infrastructure Ltd and Energía Solar Luxembourg Sarl v Kingdom of Spain* (ICSID Case No ARB/13/36) (Award dated 4 May 2017); *Novenergia II – Energy & Environment (SCA), SICAR v Kingdom of Spain* (SCC Case No 063/2015) (Award dated 15 February 2018); *Masdar Solar & Wind Cooperatief UA v Kingdom of Spain* (ICSID Case No ARB/14/1) (Award dated 16 May 2018); *Antin Infrastructure Services Luxembourg Sàrl and Antin Energia Termosolar BV v Kingdom of Spain* (ICSID Case No ARB/13/31) (Award dated 15 June 2018); *Foresight Luxembourg Solar 1 Sarl, Foresight Luxembourg Solar 2 Sarl, Greentech Energy System A/S, GWM Renewable Energy I SPA and GWM Renewable Energy II SPA v Kingdom of Spain* (SCC Case No 2015/150) (Award dated 14 November 2018); *RREEF Infrastructure (GP) Ltd and RREEF Pan-European Infrastructure Two Lux Sarl v Kingdom of Spain* (ICSID Case No ARB/13/30) (Decision on Responsibility and on the Principles of Quantum dated 30 November 2018); *NextEra Energy Global Holdings BV and NextEra Energy Spain Holdings BV v Kingdom of Spain* (ICSID Case No ARB/14/11) (Award dated 31 May 2019); *9REN Holding Sarl v Kingdom of Spain* (ICSID Case No ARB/15/15) (Award dated 31 May 2019); *InfraRed Environmental Infrastructure GP Ltd v Kingdom of Spain* (ICSID Case No ARB/14/12) (Award dated 2 August 2019); *Cube Infrastructure Fund SICAV v Kingdom of Spain* (ICSID Case No ARB/15/20) (Award dated 15 July 2019); *SolEs Badajoz GmbH v Kingdom of Spain* (ICSID Case No ARB/15/38) (Award dated 31 July 2019); *OperaFund Eco-Invest SICAV plc and Schwab Holding AG v Kingdom of Spain* (ICSID Case No ARB/15/36) (Award dated 6 September 2019); *RWE Innogy GmbH and RWE Innogy Aersa SAU v Kingdom of Spain* (ICSID Case No ARB/14/34) (Decision on Jurisdiction, Liability and Certain Issues of Quantum dated 30 December 2019); *Watkins Holdings Sarl v Kingdom of Spain* (ICSID Case No ARB/15/44) (Award dated 21 January 2020); *Hydro Energy 1 Sarl and Hydroxana Sweden AB v Kingdom of Spain* (ICSID Case No ARB/15/42) (Decision on Jurisdiction, Liability and Directions on Quantum dated 9 March 2020); *The PV Investors v Kingdom of Spain* (PCA Case No 2012-14) (Final Award dated 28 February 2020); *Cavalum SGPS, SA v Kingdom of Spain* (ICSID Case No ARB/15/34); *JGC Corp v Kingdom of Spain* (ICSID Case No ARB/15/27) (Decision on Jurisdiction, Liability and Directions on Quantum dated 31 August 2020); *STEAG GmbH v Kingdom of Spain* (ICSID Case No ARB/15/4) (Decision on Jurisdiction, Liability and Directions dated October 2020); *Eurus Energy Holdings Corp v Kingdom of Spain* (ICSID Case No ARB/16/4) (Decision on Jurisdiction and Liability dated 17 March 2021); *RENERGY Sarl v Kingdom of Spain* (ICSID Case No ARB/14/18) (Award dated 6 May 2022); *BayWa r.e. Renewable Energy GmbH and BayWa r.e. Asset Holding GmbH v Kingdom of Spain* (ICSID Case No ARB/15/16) (Award dated 25 January 2021); *Matthias Kruck v Kingdom of Spain* (ICSID Case No ARB/15/23) (Decision on Jurisdiction, Liability and Principles of Quantum dated 14 September 2022); *Aharon Naftali Biram, Gilatz Spain SL, Redmill Holdings Ltd and Sun-Flower Olmeda GmbH v Kingdom of Spain* (ICSID Case No ARB/16/17) (Award dated 22 June 2021); *Infracapital F1 Sarl and Infracapital Solar BV v Kingdom of Spain* (ICSID Case No ARB/16/18) (Decision on Jurisdiction, Liability and Directions on Quantum dated 13 September 2021); *Cordoba Beheer BV, Cross Retail SL, Sevilla Beheer BV, Spanish Project Companies v Kingdom of Spain* (ICSID Case No ARB/16/27) (Decision on Jurisdiction, Liability and the Principles of Quantum dated 11 February 2022); *Canepa Green Energy Opportunities I, Sarl and Canepa Green Energy Opportunities II, Sarl v Kingdom of Spain* (ICSID Case No ARB/19/4) (Decision on jurisdiction,

admissibility, liability and general directions with respect to quantum dated 30 October 2023); *E.ON SE, E.ON Finanzanlagen GmbH and E.ON Iberia Holding GmbH v Kingdom of Spain* (ICSID Case No ARB/15/35) (Award dated 18 January 2024); *Cavalum SGPS, SA v Kingdom of Spain* (ICSID Case No ARB/15/34) (Award dated 29 September 2022); *EDF Energies Nouvelles SA v Spain* (PCA Case No AA613) (Award dated April 2023); and *Mitsui & Co Ltd v Kingdom of Spain* (ICSID Case No ARB/20/47) (Decision on jurisdiction, liability and principles of quantum dated 31 May 2024).
58 See, eg, *Masdar Solar & Wind Cooperatief UA v Kingdom of Spain* (ICSID Case No ARB/14/1) (Award dated 16 May 2018).
59 See, eg, *Eiser Infrastructure Ltd and Energía Solar Luxembourg Sarl v Kingdom of Spain* (ICSID Case No ARB/13/36) (Award dated 4 May 2017); *Novenergia II – Energy & Environment (SCA), SICAR v Kingdom of Spain* (SCC Case No 063/2015) (Award dated 15 February 2018); and *Hydro Energy 1 Sarl and Hydroxana Sweden AB v Kingdom of Spain* (ICSID Case No ARB/15/42) (Decision on Jurisdiction, Liability and Directions on Quantum dated 9 March 2020).
60 See, eg, *Blusun SA, Jean-Pierre Lecorcier and Michael Stein v Italian Republic* (ICSID Case No ARB/14/3); *Belenergia SA v Italian Republic* (ICSID Case No ARB/15/40); *Eskosol SPA in liquidazione v Italian Republic* (ICSID Case No ARB/15/50); *Sun Reserve Luxco Holdings SRL v Italy* (SCC Case No 132/2016); *CEF Energia BV v Italian Republic* (SCC Case No 158/2015); *Greentech Energy Systems A/S, NovEnergia II Energy & Environment (SCA) SICAR, and NovEnergia II Italian Portfolio SA v Italian Republic* (SCC Case No 2015/095); *ESPF Beteiligungs GmbH, ESPF Nr. 2 Austria Beteiligungs GmbH and InfraClass Energie 5 GmbH & Co KG v Italian Republic* (ICSID Case No ARB/16/5); *Silver Ridge Power BV v Italy* (ICSID Case No ARB/15/37); *CIC Renewable Energies Italy GmbH, Enernovum Asset 1 GmbH & Co KG, Enernovum GmbH & Co KG v Italian Republic* (ICSID Case No ARB/16/39); *Encavis v Italian Republic* (ICSID Case No ARB/20/39); *Veolia Propreté SAS v Italy* (ICSID Case No ARB/18/20); and *Hamburg Commercial Bank AG v Italy* (ICSID Case No ARB/20/3).
61 The following cases were awarded in favour of the investor: *CEF Energia BV v Italian Republic* (SCC Case No 158/2015) (Award dated 16 January 2019); *Greentech Energy Systems A/S, NovEnergia II Energy & Environment (SCA) SICAR, and NovEnergia II Italian Portfolio SA v Italian Republic* (SCC Case No 2015/095) (Final Award dated 23 December 2018); *ESPF Beteiligungs GmbH, ESPF Nr. 2 Austria Beteiligungs GmbH and InfraClass Energie 5 GmbH & Co KG v Italian Republic* (ICSID Case No ARB/16/5) (Award dated 14 September 2020). The following claims were awarded in favour of the state: *Blusun SA, Jean-Pierre Lecorcier and Michael Stein v Italian Republic* (ICSID Case No ARB/14/3) (Award dated 27 December 2016); *Belenergia SA v Italian Republic* (ICSID Case No ARB/15/40) (Award dated 6 August 2019); *Eskosol SPA in liquidazione v Italian Republic* (ICSID Case No ARB/15/50) (Award dated 4 September 2020); *Sun Reserve Luxco Holdings SRL v Italy* (SCC Case No 132/2016) (Award dated 25 March 2020); *Silver Ridge Power BV v Italy* (ICSID Case No ARB/15/37) (Award dated 26 February 2021).
62 *Global Arbitration Review*, "Czech Republic wins first solar case" (13 October 2017), https://globalarbitrationreview.com/article/1148951/czech-republic-wins-first-solar-case.
63 See, eg, *Voltaic Network GmbH v Czech Republic* (PCA Case No 2014-20); *Photovoltaik Knopf Betriebs GmbH v Czech Republic* (PCA Case No 2014-21); *JSW Solar (zwei) GmbH & Co KG, Gisela Wirtgen, Jürgen Wirtgen and Stefan Wirtgen v Czech Republic* (PCA Case No 2014-03); *ICW Europe Investments Ltd v Czech Republic* (PCA Case No 2014-22); *WA Investments-Europa Nova Ltd v Czech Republic* (PCA Case No 2014-19); *Antaris Solar GmbH and Dr Michael Göde v Czech Republic* (PCA Case No 2014-01); and *GIHG Ltd, Natland Group Ltd, Natland Investment Group NV, and Radiance Energy Holding SARL v Czech Republic* (PCA Case No 2013-35).
64 See, eg, *Voltaic Network GmbH v Czech Republic* (PCA Case No 2014-20) (Award dated 15 May 2019); *Photovoltaik Knopf Betriebs GmbH v Czech Republic* (PCA Case No 2014-21) (Award dated 15 May 2019); *JSW Solar (zwei) GmbH & Co KG, Gisela Wirtgen, Jürgen Wirtgen and Stefan Wirtgen v Czech Republic* (PCA Case No 2014-03) (Award dated 11 October 2017); *ICW Europe Investments Ltd v Czech Republic* (PCA Case No 2014-22) (Award dated 15 May 2019); *WA Investments-Europa Nova Ltd v Czech Republic* (PCA Case No 2014-19) (Award dated 15 May 2019); and *Antaris Solar GmbH and Dr Michael Göde v Czech Republic* (PCA Case No 2014-01) (Award dated 2 May 2018).
65 See, eg, *GIHG Ltd, Natland Group Ltd, Natland Investment Group NV and Radiance Energy Holding SARL v Czech Republic* (PCA Case No 2013-35). The seventh, and final, case instituted against the Czech Republic has been suspended, but media reports suggest that a partial award issued by the tribunal in 2017 found a breach of the FET standard: Cosmo Sanderson, "Four more solar wins for Czech Republic", *Global Arbitration Review* (17 May 2019), https://globalarbitrationreview.com/article/1193104/four-more-solar-wins-for-czech-republic.
66 See eg, *Aderlyne Limited v Romania* (ICSID Case No ARB/22/13); *KELAG-Kärntner Elektrizitäts-Aktiengesellschaft and others v Romania* (ICSID Case No ARB/21/54); *EP Wind Project (Rom) Six Ltd v Romania* (ICSID Case No ARB/20/15); *Fin.Doc S.r.l., Domenica Gazineo, En.Doc Srl and others v Romania* (ICSID Case No ARB/20/35); and *LSG Building Solutions GmbH and others v Romania* (ICSID Case No ARB/18/19).
67 *Global Arbitration Review*, "Romania faces ICSID claim over cuts to renewable energy incentives" (13 June 2018), https://globalarbitrationreview.com/article/romania-faces-icsid-claim-over-cuts-renewable-energy-incentives.
68 *LSG Building Solutions GmbH and others v Romania* (ICSID Case No ARB/18/19) (Decision on Jurisdiction, Liability and Principles of Reparation dated 11 July 2022).
69 *Strabag SE, Erste Nordsee-Offshore Holding GmbH and Zweite Nordsee-Offshore Holding GmbH v Federal Republic of Germany* (ICSID Case No ARB/19/29); *Mainstream Renewable Power Ltd and others v Federal Republic of Germany* (ICSID Case No ARB/21/26).

70 *Slovak Republic v Achmea BV*, C-284/16.
71 *Republic of Moldova v Komstroy LLC* (Case C-741/19), Judgment of the Court of Justice of the European Union (Grand Chamber) (2 September 2021); *Poland v PL Holdings Sàrl* (Case C-109/20).
72 See, however, *Green Power Partners K/S & anor v The Kingdom of Spain* (SCC Arbitration V (2016/135)) (Award dated 16 June 2022), in which a tribunal in an SCC arbitration seated in Stockholm declined jurisdiction over an intra-EU dispute on the basis that the arbitration clause was incompatible with EU law.
73 Eg, the Svea Court of Appeal set aside the award in *Novenergia II v Spain* on 13 December 2022; Luxembourg's Court of Cassation dismissed an enforcement action in *Micula v Romania* on 14 July 2022, holding that the dispute was not arbitrable.
74 Craig Tevendale and Samantha Bakstad, "Upstream oil and gas disputes", in Maxi Scherer (ed), *International Arbitration in the Energy Sector* (Oxford University Press, 2018), para 2.17.
75 The standardised contracts include: a power purchase agreement; an implementation agreement; an O&M agreement; a supply agreement; an installation agreement; and a finance term sheet: Open Solar Contracts, https://opensolarcontracts.org/.
76 renews.biz, "New standard contract for offshore wind projects launched" (27 November 2023), https://renews.biz/89713/new-standard-contract-for-offshore-wind-projects-launched/.
77 The anticipated publication date is the end of 2025. *Infrastructure Global*, "Work begins on new FIDIC contract for offshore wind farm projects" (4 July 2023), https://infra.global/work-begins-on-new-fidic-contract-for-offshore-wind-farm-projects/.
78 However, renewable energy can also be exported internationally. For example, Morocco is already exporting solar power to Europe via two links with Spain and has plans to expand its power exports: Climatech MEA, "Europe Rushing to Install Giant Solar & Wind farms in north Africa" (25 February 2023), www.climatechmea.com/article/europe-solar-africa.
79 Concerns about offshore wind projects have also been raised with respect to risk of collision with birds and bats, electromagnetic fields impacting animals that use the Earth's magnetic field for navigation and hunting, and sediment transport: Tethys, "Offshore Wind", https://tethys.pnnl.gov/technology/offshore-wind.
80 *Windstream Energy LLC v Government of Canada* (PCA Case No 2013-22) (Award dated 27 September 2016); *cf Mesa Power Group LLC v Government of Canada* (PCA Case No 2012-17), where similar claims were dismissed (Award dated 24 March 2016).
81 Ontario Newsroom, "Ontario Rules out Offshore Wind Projects" (11 February 2011), https://news.ontario.ca/en/release/16973/ontario-rules-out-offshore-wind-projects.
82 IEA, "World Energy Investment 2024", *supra*, p67; *The Guardian*, "Ørsted cancels two US offshore windfarm projects at £3.3bn cost" (1 November 2023), www.theguardian.com/environment/2023/nov/01/rsted-cancels-two-us-offshore-windfarm-projects-at-33bn-cost; BBC News, "What does the scrapping of a wind farm plan mean for UK renewable energy?" (22 July 2023), www.bbc.co.uk/news/uk-england-norfolk-66267860#:~:text=Work%20has%20stopped%20on%20one,the%20UK%27s%20renewable%20energy%20industry%3F.
83 G20 Anti-Corruption Working Group, "G20 Indonesia 2022 Background Note on Mitigating Corruption Risks in Renewable Energy", 2022, www.unodc.org/documents/corruption/G20-Anti-Corruption-Resources/Thematic-Areas/Sectors/2022_Background_Note_on_Mitigating_Corruption_Risk_in_Renewable_Energy_adopted.pdf.
84 *Australasian Centre for Corporate Responsibility v Santos Ltd* (Claim no NSD858/2021).
85 Ashurst LLP, "Quickguides: International Investment Protection" (19 February 2020), www.ashurst.com/en/insights/quickguide-international-investment-protection/.
86 *MT Højgaard A/S v E.On Climate & Renewables UK Robin Rigg East Limited and another* [2017] UKSC 59.
87 *Cavendish Square Holding BV v Talal El Makdessi* [2015] UKSC 67.
88 *GPP Big Field LLP v Solar EPC Solutions SL* [2018] EWHC 2866 (Comm).
89 See, for example, *Drax Energy Solutions Ltd (formerly Haven Power Ltd) v Wipro Ltd* [2023] EWHC 1342 (TCC), where the court considered whether a liability cap provided for a single aggregate cap on the supplier's liability or multiple caps for each of the customer's claims.
90 A survey conducted by the School of International Arbitration at Queen Mary University of London (QMUL) in 2022 identified that 72% of the respondents considered arbitration to be well suited to the energy industry, and 40% prefer international arbitration to resolve energy infrastructure disputes over other types of dispute resolution. QMUL, "Future of International Energy Arbitration Survey Report" (2022), p6, www.qmul.ac.uk/arbitration/media/arbitration/docs/Future-of-International-Energy-Arbitration-Survey-Report.pdf.
91 For example, energy and construction/engineering disputes make up 45% of the ICC's caseload: ICC, "ICC Dispute Resolution 2023 Statistics" (2024), p13, https://iccwbo.org/wp-content/uploads/sites/3/2024/06/2023-Statistics_ICC_Dispute-Resolution_991.pdf; and 14% of the LCIA's caseload: London Court of International Arbitration, "Annual Casework Report 2023" (2024), p8.
92 Both the ICC and the SCC have reported an increase in commercial disputes involving renewables projects, and the SCC has reported an increase in investor–state disputes in this area: Sukma Dwi Andrina, "Green Technology Disputes in Stockholm" (Arbitration Institute of the Stockholm Chamber of Commerce, August 2019), https://sccinstitute.com/media/1059447/green-technology-disputes-in-stockholm.pdf; ICC, "Resolving Climate Change Related Disputes through Arbitration and ADR" (2019), https://iccwbo.org/content/uploads/sites/3/2019/11/icc-arbitration-adr-commission-report-on-resolving-climate-change-related-disputes-english-version.pdf.

93 Nigel Blackaby *et al*, *Redfern and Hunter on International Arbitration*, *supra*, para 1.01.
94 United Nations, "Status: UNCITRAL Model Law on International Commercial Arbitration (1985), with amendments as adopted in 2006", https://uncitral.un.org/en/texts/arbitration/modellaw/commercial_arbitration/status.
95 A failure to do so risks losing the right to challenge an award on this basis: Arbitration Act 1966 (UK), Section 67(1).
96 Arbitration Act 1966 (UK), Section 68.
97 *Ibid*, Section 69.
98 Arbitration Bill, HL Bill 59, Section 11: https://bills.parliament.uk/publications/54937/documents/4640.
99 Arbitration Act 1966 (UK), Section 70.
100 Nigel Blackaby *et al*, *Redfern and Hunter on International Arbitration*, *supra*, para 11.02. In a survey conducted in 2008 by QMUL, 84% of respondents indicated that the opposing party had honoured the award in full in more than 76% of cases: QMUL, "International Arbitration: Corporate attitudes and practices 2008" (2008), p4, www.arbitration.qmul.ac.uk/media/arbitration/docs/IAstudy_2008.pdf.
101 The New York Convention applies to all foreign arbitration awards, wherever they are made (Article 1(1)) – but a number of signatories have made a reservation to the effect that they will only apply the Convention to awards made in another contracting state (this is known as the 'reciprocity reservation') (Article 1(3)). Where an award is made in a state that is not a contracting party to the New York Convention, then the enforceability of that award internationally will be subject to the domestic arbitration laws of the place where enforcement is sought.
102 New York Arbitration Convention, "Contracting States – List of Contracting States", www.newyorkconvention.org/list+of+contracting+states.
103 See, eg, the European Convention on International Arbitration (1961); the Inter-American Convention on International Commercial Arbitration (1975) ('the Panama Convention'); and the ICSID Convention.
104 New York Convention, Article II.
105 'Recognition' of a foreign award refers to a court making a declaration that the award has the same status as a domestic award.
106 'Enforcement' involves using the processes of local courts to compel a party to comply with an award.
107 Article III of the New York Convention provides as follows: "Each Contracting State shall recognize arbitral awards as binding and enforce them in accordance with the rules of procedure of the territory where the award is relied upon, under the conditions laid down in the following articles".
108 Article V(I) of the New York Convention provides that recognition and enforcement may be refused at the request of a party where that party proves that: (a) the parties were under some incapacity, or the underlying arbitration agreement is not valid under the relevant governing law or the law of the place where the award was made; (b) the 'losing' party was not given proper notice of the appointment of the arbitrator or the arbitration proceedings, or was otherwise not able to present its case; (c) the award deals with issues that fall outside the scope of the submission to arbitration; (d) the composition of the arbitral authority, or the arbitral procedure, was not in accordance with the parties' agreement or with the law of the country where the arbitration took place; or (e) the award has not yet become binding, or has been set aside by a competent authority, in the place where the award was made." Enforcement may also be refused at the discretion of the court pursuant to Article V(2) where the subject matter of the arbitration is not capable of settlement by arbitration in accordance with the laws of the country where enforcement is sought, or recognition or enforcement of the award would be contrary to the public policy of that country.
109 See, eg, Council Regulation (EC) No 44/2001 on jurisdiction and the recognition and enforcement of judgments in civil and commercial matters (2001 Brussels Regulation); Regulation (EU) No 1215/2012 of the European Parliament and of the Council of 12 December 2012 on jurisdiction and the recognition and enforcement of judgments in civil and commercial matters (recast) (Recast Brussels Regulation); the Convention on jurisdiction and the recognition and enforcement of judgments in civil and commercial matters (Lugano Convention); and the Hague Convention on Choice of Court Agreements (Hague Convention).
110 Gary Born, *International Commercial Arbitration*, 2nd edition (Kluwer Law International, 2014), para 1.02[B][3].
111 Sixty per cent of respondents to a survey conducted by QMUL in 2022 identified the enforceability of arbitral awards as one of their main benefits: QMUL, "Future of International Energy Arbitration Survey Report", *supra*, p6; Gary Born, *International Commercial Arbitration*, *supra*, para 1.02[B][3].
112 *Ibid*, p6.
113 27% of respondents to the survey were involved in the renewable energy sector: QMUL, "International Arbitration Survey: Driving Efficiency in International Construction Disputes" (2019), p13, www.arbitration.qmul.ac.uk/research/2019/.
114 PCA, "Optional Rules for Arbitration of Disputes Relating to Natural Resources and/or the Environment" (2001), Article 8(3), https://docs.pca-cpa.org/2016/01/Optional-Rules-for-Arbitration-of-Disputes-Relating-to-the-Environment-and_or-Natural-Resources.pdf.
115 See, eg, ICC Rules 2021, Article 22; LCIA Rules 2020, Articles 14.1(ii), 14.2 and 14.5; UNCITRAL Arbitration Rules 2021, Article 17(1); SCC Rules 2023, Articles 2(1), 23 and 28(3); SCC Expedited Arbitration Rules 2023, Article 2; HKIAC Administered Arbitration Rules 2024, Article 13.1; SIAC Rules 2016, Article 19; DIAC Arbitration Rules 2022, Article 17; and ACICA Arbitration Rules 2021, Article 25.

116 See, eg, LCIA Rules 2020, Articles 19.4 and 30; SIAC Rules 2016, Articles 24.4 and 39; and HKIAC Administered Arbitration Rules 2024, Articles 22.7 and 45.
117 See, eg, ICC Rules 2021, Article 28; LCIA Rules 2020, Articles 9.13 and 25; UNCITRAL Arbitration Rules 2021, Article 26(1); SCC Rules 2023, Article 38; HKIAC Administered Arbitration Rules 2024, Article 23; SIAC Rules 2016, Article 30.1; DIAC Arbitration Rules 2022, Appendix II, Article 1; Swiss Rules 2021, Article 29; and ACICA Arbitration Rules 2021, Article 37.
118 See, eg, ICC Rules 2021, Article 29.7; LCIA Rules 2020, Article 25.3; UNCITRAL Arbitration Rules 2021, Article 26(9); SCC Rules 2023, Article 38(5); HKIAC Administered Arbitration Rules 2024, Article 23.9; SIAC Rules 2016, Article 30.3; DIAC Arbitration Rules 2022, Appendix II, Article 1.13; Swiss Rules 2021, Article 29.5; and ACICA Arbitration Rules 2021, Article 37.8.
119 ICC Rules 2021, Article 28(1).
120 PCA Optional Rules for Arbitration of Disputes Relating to Natural Resources and/or the Environment, Article 26(1).
121 *Fiona Trust & Holding Corporation & others v Privalov & others* [2007] UKHL 40, paragraph 13.
122 Luke Carbon and Georgia Quick, "Alternative Dispute Resolution", in Ronnie King (ed), *Arbitration in the International Energy Industry* (Globe Law and Business, 2019), p57.
123 The concept of a turnkey contract is discussed in Chapter I.
124 *FIDC Conditions of Contract for Turnkey/EPC Projects* (*Silver Book*), 2nd edition (International Federation of Consulting Engineers, 2017), clause 21.
125 See *Wah v Grant Thornton International Ltd* [2012] EWHC 3198 (Ch).
126 See *Republic of Sierra Leone v SL Mining Ltd* [2021] EWHC 286 (Comm); and *NWA and others v NVF and others* [2021] EWHC 2666.
127 QMUL, "Future of International Energy Arbitration Survey Report", *supra*, p6.
128 See note 105, *supra*.
129 The Initial Report of the ICEA, published in 2015, found that the most important factor for respondents in selecting the seat was that the seat nation was signed up to the New York Convention: ICEA, "Dispute Resolution in the Energy Sector Initial Report" (2015), p11, www.scottisharbitrationcentre.org/wp-content/uploads/2015/05/ICEA-Dispute-Resolution-in-the-Energy-Sector-Initial-Report-Square-Booklet-Web-version.pdf.
130 QMUL, "International Arbitration Survey", *supra*", p11.
131 In 2023, for example, disputes arising from the construction/engineering and energy sectors represented 45% of all new cases registered with the ICC: ICC, "ICC Dispute Resolution 2023 Statistics", *supra*, p13.
132 ICSID also has an 'Additional Facility' which allows parties to use ICSID to administer the arbitration of their disputes where the requirements of Article 25 of the ICSID Convention are not satisfied. Disputes between a state and national of another state may be eligible for arbitration through the Additional Facility where:

- the dispute is an investment dispute where neither party is an ICSID member state or a national of such a state; or
- the dispute does not arise directly out of an investment but at least one party is an ICSID member state or a national of such state.

An agreement to arbitrate under the Additional Facility Rules is subject to approval by ICSID's Secretary General before proceedings can commence.
133 Nigel Blackaby *et al*, *Redfern and Hunter on International Arbitration*, *supra*, para 2.101.
134 Arbitration Bill, HL Bill 59, Section 1: https://bills.parliament.uk/publications/54937/documents/4640.
135 See, eg, LCIA Rules 2020, Article 22A; ICC Rules 2021, Articles 7, 8, 9 and 10; SCC Rules 2023, Articles 13 and 15; SIAC Rules 2016, Articles 7, 8 and 9; HKIAC Administered Arbitration Rules 2024, Articles 27 and 28; DIAC Arbitration Rules 2022, Articles 8 and 9; Swiss Rules 2021, Articles 6 and 7; and ACICA Arbitration Rules 2021, Articles 16 and 17.
136 See, eg, ICC Rules 2021, Article 9; LCIA Rules 2020, Articles 1.2, 2.2; SCC Rules 2023, Article 14; SIAC Rules 2016, Article 6.1; and HKIAC Administered Arbitration Rules 2024, Article 29.
137 LCIA Rules 2020, Article 22.7(iii).
138 LCIA Rules 2020, Article 30. An important exception is the ICC Rules, which provide for the Secretariat to publish unredacted copies of the awards within two years unless the parties object: ICC International Court of Arbitration, "Note to Parties and Arbitral Tribunals on the Conduct of the Arbitration under the ICC Rules of Arbitration" (1 January 2021), Section IV.C.
139 ACICA Arbitration Rules 2021, Schedule 1.
140 DIAC Arbitration Rules 2022, Appendix II, Article 2.
141 HKIAC Administered Arbitration Rules 2024, Schedule 4.
142 ICC Rules 2021, Article 29 and Appendix V. These provisions do not apply to the following: arbitration agreements concluded before 1 January 2012; where the parties have opted out; and where the arbitration agreement arises from a treaty (ie, investor–state arbitrations): ICC Rules 2021, Article 29(6).
143 LCIA Rules 2020, Article 9B.
144 SCC Arbitration Rules 2023, Appendix II.
145 SIAC Rules 2016, Article 30 and Schedule 1.
146 Swiss Rules 2021, Article 43.
147 See, eg, SCC Arbitration Rules 2023, Appendix II, Article 8(1) (five days); LCIA Rules 2020, Article 9.8 (14 days); ICC Rules 2021, Appendix V, Article 6(4) (15 days); SIAC Rules 2016, Schedule 1, Article 9 (14 days); HKIAC Administered Arbitration Rules 2024, Schedule 4, Article 12 (14 days); Swiss Rules 2021, Article 43(7) (15 days); and ACICA Arbitration Rules 2021, Schedule 1, Article 3.1 (five days).

148 See, eg, ICC Rules 2021, Article 29.3; LCIA Rules 2020, Article 9.11; SCC Arbitration Rules 2023, Appendix II, Article 9(5); SIAC Rules 2016, Schedule 1, Article 10; Swiss Rules 2021, Article 43(10); and ACICA Arbitration Rules 2021, Schedule 1, Article 4.3.
149 SCC Expedited Arbitration Rules 2023, Article 43.
150 For arbitration agreements concluded on or after 1 March 2017 and before 1 January 2021, the threshold for automatic application of Expedited Procedure Rules is US$2 million: ICC Rules 2021, Appendix VI, Article 1(2).
151 ICC Rules 2021, Article 30 and Appendix VI.
152 SIAC Rules 2016, Article 5.
153 ICC, "ICC Dispute Resolution 2023 Statistics", *supra*, p14.
154 Sukma Dwi Andrina, "Green Technology Disputes in Stockholm" (Arbitration Institute of the Stockholm Chamber of Commerce, August 2019), p15, https://sccinstitute.com/media/1059447/green-technology-disputes-in-stockholm.pdf.
155 For example, Articles 14.5 and 14.6 of the LCIA Rules 2020 give the tribunal broad procedural powers with regard to the fair, efficient and expeditious conduct of the arbitration, which may include truncation of the timetable.
156 SCC Arbitration Rules 2023, Article 39.
157 ICC International Court of Arbitration, "Note to Parties and Arbitral Tribunals on the Conduct of the Arbitration under the ICC Rules of Arbitration" (1 January 2021), Section VI.C.
158 SIAC Rules 2016, Article 29.
159 HKIAC Administered Arbitration Rules 2024, Article 43.
160 LCIA Rules 2020, Articles 14.6(vi) and 22.1(viii).
161 Harsh Hari Haran, "Big Data – the Key to Unlocking Arbitrator Appointments", in Carlos González-Bueno (ed), *40 Under 40 International Arbitration* (2024), (Dykinson SL, 2024).
162 IBA Rules, Article 3(1).
163 *Ibid*, Article 3(3).
164 Chartered Institute of Arbitrators, "Protocol for E-Disclosure in International Arbitration", www.ciarb.org/media/ov2ldpbw/6-managing-arbitrations-and-procedural-orders-2015.pdf (see Appendix II).
165 *Ibid*, Preamble.
166 *Ibid*, Article 1.2.
167 *Ibid*, Article 1.3(vii).
168 Article 19(5) of the Swiss Rules 2021 provides that the tribunal may (with the agreement of the parties) take steps to facilitate the settlement of the dispute before it. Appendix 4 of the ICC Rules 2021 recommends that arbitrators actively encourage parties to consider alternative dispute resolution and settlement of all or part of their case.
169 A memorial approach requires a party to produce all documents on which they will rely, as well as supporting witness and expert evidence, at the same time as their legal submissions. A memorial approach differs from a staged approach, where legal submissions are exchanged before documentary evidence and then factual and expert evidence is produced.
170 IBA Rules, Article 5.
171 See, eg, ICC Rules 2021, Article 25(3); IBA Rules, Article 6; LCIA Rules 2020, Article 21.1; PCA Optional Rules for Arbitration of Disputes Relating to Natural Resources and/or the Environment, Article 27(1); UNCITRAL Arbitration Rules 2013, Article 29.1; SCC Arbitration Rules 2023, Article 34; SIAC Rules 2016, Article 26.1; HKIAC Administered Arbitration Rules 2024, Article 25; DIAC Arbitration Rules 2022, Article 28; Swiss Rules 2021, Article 28; and ACICA Arbitration Rules 2021, Article 36.
172 The valuation date is the date on which the value of the claimant's investment is assessed for the purposes of determining compensation.
173 Asset-based approaches generally involve determining the value of a project by reference to the value of its individual assets.
174 Market-based approaches determine the market value of a project by reference to comparable projects where the market value is known or can be determined.
175 Income-based approaches broadly involve estimating the current value of future cash flows and monetary benefits lost by the claimant due to the respondent's breach, and include the discounted cash flow method.
176 *Paccar Inc v Road Haulage Association Ltd* [2023] UKSC 28.
177 See, eg, ICC Rules 2021, Article 33; LCIA Rules 2020, Article 26.9; UNCITRAL Arbitration Rules 2021, Article 36(1); SCC Arbitration Rules 2023, Article 45(1); HKIAC Administered Arbitration Rules 2024, Article 37.2(a); DIAC Arbitration Rules 2022, Article 33.1; Swiss Rules 2021, Article 36.1; and ACICA Arbitration Rules 2021, Article 44.1.
178 For a discussion of the use of facilitation and conciliation, see Luke Carbon and Georgia Quick, "Alternative Dispute Resolution", in Ronnie King (ed), *Arbitration in the International Energy Industry* (Globe Law and Business, 2019), pp51–53.
179 Campaign for Greener Arbitrations, www.greenerarbitrations.com.
180 Ashurst LLP, "Powering Change: Technologies fuelling the future", *supra*, Chapter 1, p12.
181 IEA, "Global Hydrogen Review 2023" (2023), Executive Summary, p11, www.iea.org/reports/global-hydrogen-review-2023.
182 UNEP, "Global Resources Outlook 2024" (2024), Chapter 1, p35, www.unep.org/resources/Global-Resource-Outlook-2024.
183 UNEP, "Emissions Gap Report 2023", *supra*, Executive Summary, ppxxv–xxvi.

184 UNEP, "Production Gap Report 2023" (2023), Introduction, p12, https://productiongap.org/.
185 *Ibid*, p7.
186 For example, BIMCO has developed a standard form contract for the decommissioning of offshore assets: www.bimco.org/contracts-and-clauses/bimco-contracts/dismantlecon#.
187 *Rockhopper Exploration Plc, Rockhopper Italia SPA and Rockhopper Mediterranean Ltd v Italian Republic*, *supra*.
188 IEA, "Analysing the impacts of Russia's invasion of Ukraine on energy markets and energy security", www.iea.org/topics/russias-war-on-ukraine.
189 UNEP, "Global Resources Outlook 2024", *supra*, Foreword, pix.
190 IEA, "Mineral requirements for clean energy transitions", www.iea.org/reports/the-role-of-critical-minerals-in-clean-energy-transitions/mineral-requirements-for-clean-energy-transitions.
191 *El País*, "Mexico's López Obrador moves ahead with his crusade for lithium, revoking nine concessions from Ganfeng Lithium, a Chinese firm", 26 September 2023, https://english.elpais.com/international/2023-09-26/mexicos-lopez-obrador-moves-ahead-with-his-crusade-for-lithium-revoking-nine-concessions-from-ganfeng-lithium-a-chinese-firm.html#.
192 IBA, "Achieving Justice and Human Rights in an Era of Climate Disruption" (July 2014), www.ibanet.org/MediaHandler?id=0f8cee12-ee56-4452-bf43-cfcab196cc04.

About the authors

Emma Johnson
Partner, Ashurst LLP
emma.johnson@ashurst.com

Emma Johnson is an international arbitration practitioner and advocate, and a partner at Ashurst in London. She has been listed as a 'Next Generation Partner' in *The Legal 500* since 2019. She is also listed as a 'Rising Star' in *The Legal 500*'s international arbitration power list, as 'Up and Coming' in *Chambers & Partners' UK Guide for International Arbitration* and in *Who's Who Legal.*

Emma is qualified in England and Wales. She has experience advising on arbitrations under all of the major arbitral rules, and has particular experience of advising on energy and renewables disputes, arbitrations seated in or subject to the laws of Scandinavia, and African disputes. She has regularly worked as co-counsel alongside counsel from other firms and has conducted advocacy before both civil and common law tribunals.

Emma also has public international law experience, having acted in proceedings for and against states, both under the ICSID Convention and before the International Court of Justice.

Emma is a member of the ICC's UK Arbitration and ADR Committee. She is a member of the London Court of International Arbitration (LCIA), the Chartered Institute of Arbitrators (CIArb), the International Chamber of Commerce Young Arbitrators Forum (ICC YAF), the London Court of Arbitration Young International Arbitration Group (LCIA YIAG), the Arbitration Institute of the Stockholm Chamber of Commerce – Young Arbitrators Sweden (SCC YAS), the Swiss Arbitration Association – ASA below 40, Young ICSID, the Energy Arbitration Club and Arbitral Women.

Lucy McKenzie
Senior associate, Ashurst LLP
lucy.mckenzie@ashurst.com

Lucy McKenzie is a senior associate in Ashurst's dispute resolution practice in London. Lucy's focus is the resolution of construction and infrastructure disputes for clients in the energy industry. In the renewable energy sector, her recent experience includes acting in disputes involving a CSP plant, onshore and offshore wind farms, biomass projects and energy-from-waste projects. She also works with clients in the oil and gas and natural gas industries. Lucy has acted in international and domestic arbitrations, litigations, adjudications and mediations. She has acted in international arbitrations conducted under the ICC, LCIA, UNCITRAL and ICSID Rules and performs her own advocacy.

Matthew Saunders
Partner, Ashurst LLP
matthew.saunders@ashurst.com

Matthew Saunders is a partner in Ashurst's global international arbitration practice, based in London. Matthew is qualified in England and Wales and specialises in arbitration relating to international projects in the energy and resources sectors, with a particular focus on the gas sector. He has extensive experience in arbitrating renewable energy disputes.

He has advised a broad range of clients, including sovereign and federal governments, international energy businesses, multinational corporations and financial institutions. He is a member of the London Court of International Arbitration (LCIA), the Chartered Institute of Arbitrators (CIArb) and the Association of International Energy Negotiators (AIEN). He is vice chair of the City of London Law Society International Arbitration Committee.

For further information about Ashurst's International Arbitration team, visit:

About Globe Law and Business

Globe Law and Business was established in 2005. From the very beginning, we set out to create legal books that are sufficiently high level to be of real use to the experienced professional, yet still accessible and easy to navigate. Most of our authors are drawn from Magic Circle and other top commercial firms, both in the United Kingdom and internationally.

Our titles are carefully produced, with the utmost attention paid to editorial, design and production processes. We hope this results in high-quality publications that are easy to read and a pleasure to own.

In 2021, we were very pleased to announce the start of a new chapter for Globe Law and Business following the acquisition of law books under the imprint Ark Publishing. Our law firm management list is now significantly expanded with many well-known and loved Ark Publishing titles.

We are also pleased to announce the launch of our online content platform, Globe Law Online, which allows for easy access across firms. Details of all titles included can be found at www.globelawonline.com. Email glo@globelawandbusiness.com for further details and to arrange a free trial for you or your firm.

We'd very much like to hear from you with your thoughts and ideas for improving what we offer. Please do feel free to email me at sian@globelawandbusiness.com. Happy reading and thank you for your time.

Sian O'Neill
Managing director
Globe Law and Business
www.globelawandbusiness.com

Milton Keynes UK
Ingram Content Group UK Ltd.
UKHW050026021224
451857UK00003B/3

9 781837 230525